THE BOOK OF
THE BRANCH

A prophetic unveiling of the Vine,
the Vein, and the Sons of Zion

ANTHONY MWANGI

Crony Trading LTD

*To the One who planted the Seed before time began
the Eternal Vine whose life flows as light, breath, and covenant.*

*To Jesus Christ,
the Vein of God,
the Pathway of Blood and Truth,
the Living Root from whom all sons draw strength, identity, and
fire.*

*To the Holy Spirit,
the Rest of God,
the Sabbath within the soul,
the Breath who awakens branches into full maturity.*

*To Zion,
the mountain of counsel,
the courtroom of kings,
the sanctuary where sons learn to rule.*

*And to every hidden son scattered across the nations
those who feel the quiet pull in the spirit,
those who know they were born to bear fruit in a barren age,
those whose hearts bend toward the whisper of destiny, this
book is for you.*

*May the Vine steady you.
May the Vein strengthen you.
May the Branch arise in you.*

— Anthony Mwangi — the BRANCH seated in Zion

"I am the vine, ye are the branches."
— John 15:5 (KJV)

"Out of Zion, the perfection of beauty, God hath shined."
— Psalm 50:2 (KJV)

SABBATH FIRE

CONTENTS

FOREWORD

There are books that inform, and there are books that awaken. This one does both, while building an interior architecture strong enough to host the counsel of God.

THE BOOK OF THE BRANCH is not another exploration of identity; it is an unveiling of origin. It pulls the reader out of surface-level spirituality and positions them inside the eternal blueprint—the Vine, the Vein, and the Branch as the tri-fold pattern of God's intention.

From the first chapter to the final charge, the message is clear: heaven measures sons not by their activity, but by their alignment.
The Vine is the intelligence.
The Vein is the transmission.
The Branch is the manifestation.

This is the ecosystem of divine identity.

What Anthony Mwangi—**the BRANCH seated in Zion,** has accomplished in these pages is rare. He has distilled revelation without diluting its fire. He has framed eternal truths in language accessible enough for the hungry and weighty enough for the seasoned. He has gathered ancient pathways and future assignments under one prophetic canopy.

You will notice something as you read: the tone is not coaxing; it is commissioning.
The content is not commentary; it is construction.
The invitation is not to understand more, but to **become** more.

Every page is engineered to shift posture, to take the reader from survival to sovereignty, from confusion to clarity, from fragmentation to fruitfulness.

This foreword exists for one reason: to prepare you for the gravity of what comes next.

If you approach this book casually, it will feel poetic.
If you approach this book intentionally, it will feel architectural.
If you approach this book prophetically, it will feel like Zion opening its gates.

You are holding a manual of emergence; a briefing for sons growing into their inheritance, a roadmap for branches rising into full expression, a call to align with the Vine in an hour when the world is starving for true fruit.

Read slowly.
Read prayerfully.
Read with the expectation that something ancient in you is about to stand upright.

Because once the Branch awakens, nothing stays the same.

INTRODUCTION

When the Root Speaks,
Everything Grows

Before the world began, God planted a mystery in the eternal soil:
a Sonship hidden in Christ,
a kingdom embedded in blood,
a lineage destined to bloom at the appointed time.

Creation itself is a vineyard.
The universe is the field.
Eden was the first garden.
Calvary was the great pruning.
Pentecost was the sap rising again.
And Zion is the mountain where branches mature.

Humanity was never designed to survive; we were designed to **abide**.

Abiding is not passivity; abiding is governance.
It is the strategy of those who understand how heaven flows.

To abide is to remain aligned with the original architecture of God.

In this book, we journey through three prophetic pillars:

1. **The Vine — Christ as the Source, Root, and Intelligence of**

Life

2. **The Vein — His blood as the covenant pathway of identity and power**

3. **The Branch — the sons of Zion, raised to bear fruit in an age of collapse**

Each chapter speaks into the core of your spiritual structure, calling you to rise, to stabilise, to build, to govern.

Not by striving, but by abiding.

Not by force, but by flow.

Not through institutions, but through identity.

This is the era of emergence.
The days when hidden branches rise into full expression.
The season when Zion's sons stand as living witnesses of the Vine.

Turn the page.
The unveiling begins.

PREFACE

This book did not begin with an idea.
It began with a pull.

A gravity in the spirit.
A summons from Zion.
A whisper that said, *"Trace the Vine, follow the Vein, call forth the sons."*

The deeper I went, the clearer it became:
identity is not discovered; identity is revealed.
And revelation is not information; revelation is inheritance.

This project was not written to entertain the curious.
It was crafted to architect the courageous; those who sense that the age is shifting, and that God is calling His branches back to their original blueprint.

The Vine is Christ.
The Vein is His blood; His covenant, His Spirit, His nature.
The Branch is the son: rooted in eternity, awakened in time, appointed to bear fruit in the last days.

Consider this book a framework, a map, a prophetic briefing.
It is designed to strengthen your internal architecture,
align your identity with heaven's metrics, and position you to operate as a branch fully seated in Zion.

What follows is not commentary.
It is construction.

PROLOGUE

Before the rise of mountains, before the breath of Adam, before the first pulse of time, there was a quiet.
Not emptiness—intention.
Not silence—counsel.

In that eternal stillness, God conceived a mystery:
a Vine that would carry His life,
a Vein that would carry His blood,
a Branch that would carry His name.

Creation unfolded in response to this desire.
Light came because the Root spoke.
Order emerged because the Root envisioned.
Life multiplied because the Root poured itself into the soil of time.

Every star is a seed of that first intention.
Every angel a witness to that first architecture.
Every human spirit a branch waiting to awaken.

But the story did not begin on earth.
The story began in the heart of God.

The Vine was appointed before worlds were framed.
The Vein—His blood, His covenant, His Spirit—was prepared before sin had a name.
The Branch—the sons of Zion; were chosen before flesh found form.

The earth was simply the vineyard where the revelation would bloom.

When Adam fell, the Vine remained.
When nations scattered, the Vein still flowed.
When darkness covered the earth, the Branch was hidden but never lost.

History has not been the story of man searching for God.
History has been the story of God preparing His sons.

The prophets saw it dimly.
The psalmists sang of it in fragments.
Jesus announced it openly:
"I am the vine, ye are the branches."

This book is the unveiling of that eternal ecosystem.
It is a return to the architecture that predates chaos.
A realignment with a life older than death.
A reconnection to the bloodline that cannot be corrupted.

This is not a call to religion; it is a call to inheritance.

Not to behave better; but to become who the Root intended.

Not to reach for God; but to abide in what He already established.

In these pages, the ancient blueprint emerges.
The Vine stands in full radiance.
The Vein pulses with covenant fire.
The Branch rises with the dignity of Zion.

The hour of hiddenness has ended.
The season of revealing has begun.

The Root is speaking again.
And when the Root speaks; everything grows.

PART I — THE GOLDEN ORIGIN

THE BRANCH IN THE LAMP OF GOD (Exodus 25–37)

Theme: The Pattern of the Spirit's Body

"Three bowls made like unto almonds, with a knop and a flower in one branch… so in the six branches that come out of the candlestick." — Exodus 25:33

The revelation of The Branch begins not with a tree in Eden but with a lamp in the Sanctuary. Before the seed touched soil, the pattern existed in gold — beaten, pure, and luminous. The golden candlestick reveals that the Body of the Spirit is not made but formed through pressure, unity, and eternal light.

CHAPTER 1

The Golden Blueprint

"And thou shalt make a candlestick of pure gold: of beaten work shall the candlestick be made; his shaft, and his branches, his bowls, his knops, and his flowers, shall be of the same." — Exodus 25:31

1. The Beaten Body of Light

The first revelation of the Branch was not wood, but gold. Before leaf or root appeared on earth, heaven showed Moses a living pattern: a single shaft of beaten gold, branching six ways, burning with seven lights. The lamp was not assembled; it was hammered from one piece — unity through pressure. Every blow shaped light into form, until the image of the Spirit's body emerged.

The candlestick was the Spirit made visible, the Body of Christ in type; divine essence beaten into manifest order.

2. The Pattern of the Spirit's Body

Six branches plus one shaft equals seven currents of divine operation. Each branch carried its own bowls, knops, and flowers; intelligence, strength, and beauty woven together. From one root of gold, the Spirit expressed seven natures; from one Vine, seven flames rose.

This was not furniture; it was prophecy in metal. The Spirit of the Branch would one day dwell in human temples, burning through the circuits of a redeemed mind.

3. The Sevenfold Flow: From Wisdom to Burning

The lamp's light flows like breath, from the first spark of Wisdom to the last seal of Fire. It is the full journey of divine life moving through the Body.

1. **Spirit of Wisdom** — *Light revealed.*
   She designs the pattern of thought, aligning man's mind to heaven's geometry.
   The uppermost branch where revelation first blooms.

2. **Spirit of Understanding** — *Light interpreted.*
   It translates divine pattern into language, forming parables and insight within the soul.

3. **Spirit of Counsel** — *Light governed.*
   The mind of purpose; the strategist of the Spirit who orders steps and seasons.

4. **Spirit of Might** — *Light enforced.*
   Strength that sustains obedience. The energy that endures the beating until gold becomes mirror.

5. **Spirit of Knowledge** — *Light imparted.*
   The infilling of revelation oil; to know as we are known.

6. **Spirit of Fear of the LORD** — *Light guarded.*
   The holy boundary around glory. It preserves purity so that power does not corrupt.

7. **Spirit of Judgment and Burning** — *Light perfected.*
   The consuming fire that completes the circuit, purging

mixture and sealing the vessel in holiness.

From Wisdom to Burning the Spirit moves; revelation to transformation, sight to flame. When the cycle closes, the Branch shines as pure gold, reflecting the image of the Vine.

4. The Almond Mystery

Every branch of the candlestick held bowls shaped like almonds. The almond is the first tree to awaken after winter; resurrection encoded in its blossom. Aaron's rod budded with almonds to prove divine election; the candlestick bears almonds to prophesy divine resurrection. The Branch of God would one day awaken from death and cause every branch in Him to bloom again.

5. Spiritology — Gold as Divine Nature

Gold does not rust. It endures both fire and time. Its purity speaks of the Spirit's nature: incorruptible, eternal, radiant. The lamp of gold was not painted light; it *was* light.
So the Body of Christ, beaten yet unbroken, reflects the Spirit's substance within.

6. Typology — Christ the Lamp and the Body the Branches

In the Holy Place stood one lamp, yet seven flames. In heaven stands one Vine, yet countless branches. Christ is the shaft; we are the extensions of His light. The same oil flows through us; the same fire burns. What began as gold in the wilderness becomes living flesh in the new creation.

7. From Pattern to Person

The pattern on Sinai was a shadow of a Person; the Spirit manifesting in Christ and then in His Body. Every knop and flower, every bowl and branch, prefigured the order of divine operation. When the Spirit descended at Pentecost, the lamp was relit; seven flames burning now in human hearts. The tabernacle pattern had found its fulfilment in living temples of fire.

8. Conclusion — The First Branch Awakened

From Wisdom to Burning, from gold to glory; this is the genesis of the Branch. The lamp Moses saw is the same Vine Jesus revealed: "I am the Vine, ye are the branches."
The eternal light that once burned in gold now breathes through us. Every redeemed soul is a living extension of the lamp of God.

CHAPTER 2

The Branch That Bears Fire

*"And there shall come forth a rod out of
the stem of Jesse, and a Branch shall grow
out of his roots." — Isaiah 11:1*

1. The Lamp that Breathes Fire

L ight without flame is philosophy. But fire — fire is the presence of God Himself. When the lamp of gold was filled with oil, it waited for one breath: the spark that turns still gold into living flame. This is the mystery of indwelling; not fire above man, but within him. From Sinai to Pentecost, the Spirit moved from visitation to habitation, until the Branch itself began to burn from inside out.

The Spirit's fire does not consume its vessel; it consecrates it. Gold is not afraid of flame; it is purified by it. Thus, the Branch that truly lives is the one that bears fire without being destroyed.

2. The Priesthood of the Living Branch

> *"And behold, the rod of Aaron... was budded,*
> *and brought forth buds, and bloomed blossoms,*
> *and yielded almonds." — Numbers 17:8*

When rebellion rose among the tribes, God chose a sign that could not be argued; a dead rod that flowered overnight. Aaron's rod, a cut branch, suddenly bore life. It budded, bloomed, and produced almonds — resurrection, beauty, and fruit — all at once.

That rod became the priesthood's witness: life in death, authority in humility, fire in stillness. It was the *Branch within the Ark*; a hidden prophecy of Christ's priesthood and ours.

Priesthood is not a title; it is a branch that burns continually before God. Every priest carries within him that same almond miracle: the ability to bear life after dying, to bloom in a wilderness, to carry fire through holiness.

3. Physiology — The Living Body that Circulates Fire

The candlestick was a body; a golden physiology of divine circulation. Oil flowed through every branch like blood through veins, carrying fire to each lamp. Light is not static; it moves. Revelation circulates. When one branch burns brighter, the others share the same increase. In the body of the Branch, no flame is isolated; every fire is communal.

So the physiology of the Spirit is both biological and celestial; a living system of light, breath, and renewal. Every cell in the redeemed body becomes a wick, drawing oil from the Vine, releasing light to the world.

4. Chronology — The First Appearance of the Branch

The first physical appearance of the Branch pattern was not in the garden, but in the *Tabernacle*. Adam was the breath of God in dust; Moses beheld the breath of God in gold. Both were prototypes of the same mystery: the Spirit forming a vessel fit for light.

Chronologically, the candlestick marks the *first prophetic blueprint* of Christ's indwelling Spirit. Before Bethlehem, before Calvary, before Pentecost; there was a lamp burning in the wilderness, declaring:

"The Branch is coming. The fire will no longer visit; it will dwell."

That lamp was heaven rehearsing incarnation. The golden lamp was the embryo of the divine Body that would one day be born as Christ, and later multiplied as His Church; the living menorah of the earth.

5. Soulogy — The Fire of Consciousness

Within man, the mind mirrors the lamp. The intellect is the bowl; the emotions the flame; the will the wick. When oil fills the soul, thought becomes light. Every inspired idea, every holy desire, every yielded choice; fire passing through gold.

Thus, the soul becomes priestly when it agrees with divine circulation. Rebellion blocks the oil. Pride smothers the flame. But surrender — surrender makes the mind transparent to glory. That is how the fire of God travels unhindered through the inner Branch.

6. Spiritology — The Breath that Ignites

Fire begins where breath enters.
When God breathed into Adam, the dust became a lamp.
When Christ breathed on the disciples, the Church became a living menorah.
The same breath that once hovered over formless waters now dwells in human clay, kindling eternal light.

Spirit is not abstract wind; it is the fire-bearing breath of the Vine. When it enters a vessel, it carries both intelligence and intensity — wisdom and burning. The same breath that reveals also refines.

7. Theology — The Branch and the Vine

Jesus did not call Himself the branch; He called Himself the Vine. The Branch was prophetic shadow; the Vine is fulfilment. Yet the mystery deepens; the Vine, having ascended, now extends Himself again through us as the *branches*.
We are not replacements, but continuations — living extensions of His nature on earth.

When the Vine passed through death and rose, He became the eternal Source of oil. Now every branch that abides in Him shares His circulation of fire. The Branch has become the Vine; and the Vine, through us, becomes the Branch again. Thus judgment and mercy, priesthood and kingship, light and life all converge in one body; the golden candlestick of the redeemed.

8. Typology — The Lamp, the Rod, and the Cross

Three trees define redemption:

- The **Lamp** — the tree of light (Spirit indwelling)

- The **Rod** — the tree of authority (Priesthood)

- The **Cross** — the tree of judgment (Love fulfilled)

All are one Branch seen at different stages of burning. The lamp was gold, the rod was wood, the cross was both wood and fire. Each stage reveals another degree of the Spirit's embodiment, from pattern to person to power.

9. Conclusion — The Branch that Bears Fire

When the Spirit descended as tongues of fire, it was not a new event; it was the lamp of Exodus relit inside human vessels. The pattern became people. The same fire that once hovered over the golden candlestick now dwells in the hearts of flesh.
And wherever the oil flows freely, the Branch still bears fire.

The Branch lives in us.
The lamp burns through us.
The Vine breathes among us.

The fire will not go out until all the earth glows with the light of the Holy One.

PART II — THE VINE IN THE WILDERNESS

THE BRANCH TESTED AND TRIED
(Numbers–Job–Psalms–Proverbs)

CHAPTER 3

The Cluster of Eshcol

"And they came unto the brook of Eshcol, and cut down from thence a branch with one cluster of grapes, and they bare it between two upon a staff; and they brought of the pomegranates, and of the figs." (Numbers 13:23–24)

1. Spiritology — The Hidden Wine of the Spirit

Eshcol means cluster; the gathering of divine essence within one vine. This prophetic moment was not agricultural; it was spiritual. The branch from Eshcol represents the Spirit-filled Christ, the living vine whose fruit carries the wine of the covenant. Two men bore one cluster, symbolising the Law and the Prophets carrying the revelation of Christ, the hidden wine sealed in the wilderness. Every grape in that cluster carried Spirit-life compressed through suffering; the wine could not flow until it was crushed.

"I have trodden the winepress alone..." (Isaiah 63:3)

The wilderness was the winepress where the Vine was tested, and faith was fermented into maturity.

2. Soulogy — The Journey from Seeing to Tasting

The spies saw the land, saw the fruit, and carried it; but they never **tasted** it.
Sight without faith is the tragedy of the soul. The soul that only observes the promise but fears the giants cannot enter rest.
The cluster was proof, not possession. Eshcol reveals the difference between **vision and participation**, between carrying revelation and becoming one with it.

The soul must go beyond admiration to assimilation, from beholding the fruit to being filled with its life. Only when the heart drinks of the Vine does faith become experience.

3. Physiology — The Branch as the Circulatory Body of Life

The cluster was carried **between two upon a staff**; a perfect picture of Christ's crucifixion. The wood of the staff represented the cross; the cluster represented His body; the two men the dual covenantal testimony. Just as blood circulates through veins (vines) to nourish the body, so the Spirit flows through the **branches** of Christ's Body to feed every member.
The wilderness is the divine bloodstream where faith cells are purified through heat and thirst.
The Vine's physiology is built to thrive where human systems fail; it roots deep where there is no rain.

The wilderness teaches the body of the Vine how to carry glory under pressure.

4. Theology — Christ the True Eshcol

Christ is the true Cluster. From Him flows the sevenfold wine; the Spirits of Wisdom, Understanding, Counsel, Might,

Knowledge, Judgment, and Burning.
The Law and the Prophets bore Him on their shoulders through generations until He was revealed in the flesh.
The grapes symbolise the **compressed revelation of ages**, fermented by obedience, preserved by fire, and served as communion wine in the fullness of time.

Every prophet tasted a drop; every psalmist sang a sip.
But the full cup came at Calvary; the Vine poured out His life.

5. Chronology — From Promise to Pressing

- **In Numbers:** The Vine was seen in shadow (the cluster).

- **In Job:** The Vine was pressed through affliction.

- **In Psalms:** The Vine sang in worship.

- **In Proverbs:** The Vine spoke as Wisdom.
  The progression of Eshcol is a divine metamorphosis — from fruit to wine, from promise to covenant, from symbol to Spirit.

6. Typology — Christ Between Law and Prophets

The two men carrying the branch mirror **Moses and Elijah**, who later stood with Jesus on the Mount of Transfiguration. They carried the prophetic weight of redemption through generations.
The wilderness, like the human heart, tested the strength of the Vine; could it still bear fruit in barrenness?
Christ, the Vine, remained faithful where Israel fainted.
Thus, the Branch of Eshcol becomes the **prototype of the enduring Spirit**, that still bears fruit in dry seasons.

7. Technology — The Law of the Cluster

The *spiritual technology* of the cluster is union through

compression. Every grape is distinct yet connected, showing that divine fruitfulness flows through **oneness under pressure**. No grape can mature outside the cluster; no believer can mature outside the Body.

Eshcol is the system of **shared endurance**, where affliction produces corporate wine.

The more the cluster is pressed, the purer the flow. The Church becomes a living Eshcol when every member bears the weight of another's burden.

Prophetic Conclusion — The Vine in Transition

Eshcol was the threshold between wilderness and inheritance, the border between potential and possession.
Those who murmured at Eshcol rejected the Vine and returned to dryness. But those who drink from it receive the Spirit of conquest.

Declaration:

"O Vine of Life, press me until my faith ferments into wine!
Let the wilderness be the place of my ripening.
Make me a living cluster of Your Spirit, a testimony carried by angels and men."

CHAPTER 4

The Branch in the Dust (Job 8–29)

"For there is hope of a tree, if it be cut down, that it will sprout again, and that the tender branch thereof will not cease. Though the root thereof wax old in the earth, and the stock thereof die in the ground; Yet through the scent of water it will bud, and bring forth boughs like a plant." (Job 14:7–9 KJV)

1. Spiritology — Hope Beyond Affliction: Resurrection Encoded in Roots

The Spirit of Life hides resurrection in roots. Job's revelation was not from theology but from encounter; the whisper of the Vine within the soil of suffering. Though the branch was scorched, its root retained memory of water.

Hope is not born in the leaf but in the root; where the Spirit hides the law of rebirth.

When Job said, *"I know that my Redeemer liveth,"* he was prophesying the **law of spiritual resurrection**; that death can never uproot what was planted by Spirit-fire.

The Vine may appear dead above ground, but beneath the dust, the Spirit is rewriting resurrection codes. Suffering is the Spirit's language of root repair.

Gold was beaten in Exodus; the branch is broken in Job; both reveal the same mystery: the Spirit refines by pressing divine life deeper until it touches the waters of eternity.

2. Soulogy — The Soul's Awakening Through Divine Pruning

In Job's lament, we witness the **soul of man under divine surgery**. Affliction prunes perception; cutting away false leaves of pride, self-righteousness, and fear. Every pruning in the soul is designed to make space for the flow of pure sap — the Spirit's truth.

When Job's friends accused him, God allowed silence to mature his roots. True growth happens when the soul ceases to defend itself and begins to listen to the inner Vine. Thus, Job's despair became the soil where the **soul remembered Spirit**. When words failed, the Vine began to whisper within him, and hope sprouted again.

Divine pruning is not rejection; it is purification of perception. Every cut is a call to a deeper consciousness of the indwelling root.

3. Physiology — The Branch Revived by the Scent of Water

Job saw what botanists could never explain:
The scent — not the flood — awakens dead roots.
This is the physiology of resurrection: before the water reaches the roots, **the Spirit's breath announces its coming**.

The scent of water is the **frequency of the Holy Spirit** that reactivates divine DNA in the dust of man. It touches the dormant cells and commands them, *"Live again."* Even the human body, made of dust, responds to this vibration. That is why the resurrection of Christ shook graves; dust recognised the voice of its Root.

When the Spirit breathes, dry bones remember the Vine.
The body, though frail, becomes the tabernacle of renewal.

4. Theology — Job as the Typology of Christ Buried and Raised

Job is not merely a man in pain; he is a **prophetic shadow of the suffering Vine** — Christ in the dust.

- He was cut down by loss.

- Bruised by misunderstanding.

- Laid low among ashes.

- Yet rooted in faith beyond sight.

The theology of Job reveals the gospel before Calvary: that the righteous seed must die before it multiplies. Job's confession — *"Though He slay me, yet will I trust Him"* — is the cry of the eternal Vine to the Father, declaring, "I am still rooted in You."

In Job, we see Christ buried in humiliation; In Job's restoration, we see the resurrection glory of the Branch restored double.

5. Chronology — From Dust to Double Portion

Job's journey follows a divine chronology of regeneration:

1. **Dust:** The branch cut and buried (*Job 2–3*).

2. **Debate:** The pruning of perception (*Job 8–20*).

3. **Despair:** The silence before the scent of water (*Job 21–28*).

4. **Discovery:** The awakening of root-consciousness (*Job 29–37*).

5. **Deliverance:** The water reaches the root — the Vine revives

(*Job 38–42*).

Every righteous man passes through this pattern: buried in misunderstanding, watered by mercy, revived in divine sight.

6. Typology — Roots Hidden, Fruit Revealed

The branch's beauty is in its hiddenness. The unseen life beneath the soil sustains the visible. Job's faith was unseen by men but seen by God; a root tested in obscurity.
Satan struck the fruit, but could not reach the root. The dust became a veil covering divine preparation.

So too, the Church in tribulation — hidden, pressed, accused — is being rooted for the final rain. For in the end-time, the remnant Branch will bud again through the scent of the Spirit's water.

7. Technology — The Law of the Root Memory

Every living root carries **spiritual memory**. Even when cut off, it retains the blueprint of what it once was. This is the divine technology of restoration: the Spirit reawakens what is recorded in the root's design.

When God restores, He doesn't start from the leaf; He starts from the seed-memory embedded in dust. Thus, resurrection is not invention; it is remembrance. The Spirit calls the branch by name, and the root responds with new growth.

The scent of water = activation of memory.
The rain of Spirit = manifestation of renewal.
The fruit that follows = testimony of hope beyond affliction.

Prophetic Conclusion — The Branch Will Rise from the Dust

Job's testimony becomes the anthem of every generation buried by trial: *"At the scent of water it will bud."* The Spirit's whisper revives buried callings, dormant anointings, forgotten promises, and weary hearts. Dust is not the end; it is the womb of the next beginning.

Declaration:

"O Spirit of the Living God, breathe Your scent upon my dust!
Let every buried root awaken and remember its first design.
From the ashes, let the Vine bud again, until resurrection flows through every branch."

CHAPTER 5

The Branch of Strength
(Psalm 80:15)

"And the vineyard which Thy right hand hath planted,
and the branch that Thou madest strong for Thyself."

Theme: The Right Hand that Plants, the Vine that Endures

Theology — The Covenant Root:

The right hand of God is the Word in action — the creative arm of strength. What He plants, no drought uproots, it carries His own remembrance as its root. Israel was not chosen for soil but for the seed hidden in her promise in the root, for the covenant that flows through blood and word alike. The branch of strength is not man's achievement; it is God's remembrance of His oath to Himself and the fulfilment of God's self-sworn oath, living through generations as an unbroken root of mercy.

Spiritology — The Strength Hidden in Weakness:

The branch is "made strong" not by outward might, but by inward sap. Fire circulates through it unseen. The Spirit moves through the branch as unseen fire, transmuting wounds into nourishment. Every pruning becomes a pulse of resurrection. When God strengthens a branch, He does not shield it from the knife; He feeds it through the wound. Divine fire does not destroy the tender stem; it fuses it into the Vine. Resurrection is not a single act but the constant exchange between loss and life.

Soulogy — The Vineyard Within:

The heart becomes the vineyard. Every promise is a vine; every trial, a season of pressing. The soul is a field that ripens under pressure. The soul learns that strength is not the absence of breaking, but the endurance of life through it. Each promise is a vine winding through the chambers of the heart; each testing a season of pressing, where sweetness is drawn out of surrender. The strong branch is not the proud one; it's the vessel that bends without breaking, the heart that learns obedience through pruning.

Prophetic View — The Messiah Hidden in the Vineyard:

Before Christ called Himself the *True Vine*, He was this Branch "made strong for Himself" — bruised yet bearing fruit, cut yet crowned with sap that could sustain the world. In Psalm 80's cry, "Return, we beseech Thee," was a prophecy in disguise; Israel's song was unknowingly about the Son, the branch that would carry divine strength through suffering, until the Vine could carry all branches within Himself. When He rose, the Vine overtook the vineyard; the root became the tree, and the covenant took flesh.

Application:

To be a branch of strength is to let God remember Himself in you and to yield where others resist. His right hand still plants, prunes, and pours through those who remain yielded.

True power in the Spirit is not in standing alone, but in abiding unbroken in His vine. The mark of divine strength is continuity; the quiet persistence of life that refuses to die, because it no longer belongs to the one living it.

CHAPTER 6

The Flourishing Branch

"He that trusteth in his riches shall fall: but the righteous shall flourish as a branch." (Proverbs 11:28)

Theme: Prosperity that Breathes, Not Boasts

Theology — The Source of True Flourishing:

Flourishing in the kingdom is not seasonal but spiritual. The leaf withers when it trusts the weather; the branch thrives because it abides in the Vine. Riches are only temporary rivers; they dry when the heart withdraws from its Source. But righteousness, being right alignment with the life of God, draws living water from eternity. Prosperity is not possession; it is participation in divine order.

Soulogy — Dependence Versus Self-Reliance:

Self-reliance is the soul's drought. It cuts the branch from the root while pretending to stand on its own. Dependence, in the Spirit, is not weakness; it's the law of growth. Every branch that flourishes bends toward its Source. True maturity is a graceful dependence, where the soul stops managing its own fruit and lets the Vine decide the season.

Spiritology — Prosperity That Flows from Inner Righteousness:

Inward righteousness is the Spirit's equilibrium. It's the steady sap that flows from root to leaf, from obedience to manifestation. Prosperity begins as a rhythm inside the heart; peace, purity, and purpose moving together. When the Spirit rules the flow, the branch bears abundance without anxiety.

Physiology — The Circulation of Blessing:

In creation, every living thing flourishes by circulation, not hoarding. So too the righteous: what they receive, they release; what they release, returns multiplied. The Spirit keeps the flow holy by burning away fear and pride, the two diseases of fruitfulness.

Prophetic View — The Secret Economy of the Branch:

Heaven measures prosperity by continuity, not accumulation. To flourish as a branch is to remain connected, useful, and green even in famine. The righteous carry a climate of Eden within them; they bring seasons into barren lands. Their fruit is not for display but for feeding nations.

Application:

Flourishing begins where trust changes direction. The branch that stops reaching for gold and starts abiding in grace becomes unbreakable. Prosperity in the Spirit is not about *having* much, but *holding nothing* apart from the Vine.

PART III — THE PROPHETIC SHOOT

THE BRANCH FORETOLD
(Isaiah–Jeremiah–Zechariah)

CHAPTER 7

The Branch of Beauty of the LORD

"In that day shall the Branch of the LORD be beautiful and glorious, and the fruit of the earth shall be excellent and comely for them that are escaped of Israel." (Isiah 4:2)

Theme: Where Flourishing Matures into Glory

Theology — Beauty Born of Purity:

This beauty is not cosmetic; it is covenantal. The Branch of the LORD is beautiful because He has been purified by fire and found without blemish. Holiness is the hidden architecture of divine beauty; it orders the soul the way light orders creation. Glory is simply holiness unveiled.

Spiritology — The Remnant Purified for Fruitfulness:

Isaiah 4 opens with judgment but ends with a remnant washed and refined. The Branch of the LORD is the pattern for that remnant; fruitful because purified, radiant because emptied. The Spirit's fire consumes excess, not essence. Every purification is a preparation for greater beauty. Those who endure His cleansing bear fruit that reflects not self, but Spirit.

Soulogy — The Inner Garment of Glory:

The soul becomes comely when it no longer seeks to be seen. The desire to appear beautiful fades when the inner light begins to shine. True beauty is quiet authority; the calm of a heart in which God has finished His work. Glory does not decorate; it emanates.

Physiology — The Radiance of Holiness in Flesh:

When the Spirit indwells, even the body becomes an instrument of light. The face of Moses shone because holiness had found a vessel. Likewise, those who abide in the Branch begin to glow with obedience; their countenance reflects alignment. Purity is visible.

Prophetic View — The Glory of the Escaped Ones:

Isaiah says, *"for them that are escaped of Israel."* Escape is not flight but refinement; passing through fire without losing form. The escaped ones are not the proud survivors, but the surrendered remnant through whom the Lord restores Edenic beauty to the earth. The Branch of the LORD is Christ glorified; the escaped are His reflections, branches of His beauty spreading through the nations.

Application:

To mature from flourishing to glory is to let holiness finish its work. Beauty in the Spirit is not the reward of effort but the residue of surrender. When the branch stops striving to bloom and simply abides in purity, it begins to shine.

CHAPTER 8

The Rod from Jesse (Isaiah 11:1–10)

The Branch of Wisdom and Understanding —
where glory deepens into governance

1. The Root Awakening: Hidden Life in a Stump

When Isaiah saw a Rod spring forth from the stem of Jesse, he was beholding resurrection power hidden inside lineage death. Jesse's tree (the Davidic dynasty) looked cut down; Babylon had felled it, exile had silenced it, and the royal song of Zion seemed forgotten. Yet within that stump, the Root remained alive; the unseen covenant pulse of the Spirit.

> *"There shall come forth a rod out of the*
> *stem of Jesse, and a Branch shall grow out*
> *of his roots." — Isaiah 11:1 KJV*

The "rod" speaks of **authority reborn**, while the "branch" signifies **fruit-bearing wisdom**. Together they form the **staff of divine governance**, carried by the Messiah — the Spirit-governed Man.

2. Spiritology — The Sevenfold Anointing Resting on the Branch

The Spirit of the LORD did not merely visit Him — it *rested* upon Him. The Hebrew "nuach" means to dwell, to settle, to Sabbath. Thus, the Branch is **the Sabbath embodied**, the resting place of the fullness of the Spirit.

> *"And the Spirit of the LORD shall rest*
> *upon Him…" — Isaiah 11:2 KJV*

The **Spirit of the LORD** is the Holy Spirit Himself, the **Person of Dominion and Identity**, the fountainhead from whom all divine operations flow.

From Him, the sevenfold current flows — streaming outward as facets of His own being, forming the architecture of divine government.

He is the **Root Flame**, the **Crown River** of governance, the **Person of Rest** from whom every other Spirit proceeds. This is the mystery of divine channelling administration — the **one Spirit manifesting sevenfold**.

"Before the throne burned seven lamps of fire, which are the seven Spirits of God." — Revelation 4:5

From Him stream the seven currents of divine government; each a dimension of His own being, flowing from rest into rule:

1. **The Spirit of Wisdom** — Strategic comprehension of divine order; revealing divine design; the architect of eternal patterns.

2. **The Spirit of Understanding** — Perception of invisible patterns; interpreting divine structure; the key of discernment.

3. **The Spirit of Counsel** — The architecture of righteous decisions - aligning divine strategy with earthly action; the voice of divine planning.

4. **The Spirit of Might** — Strength to establish spiritual decrees; enforcing divine strength; power that sustains purity.

5. **The Spirit of Knowledge** — Experiential intimacy with divine truth; knowing as one who is known.

6. **The Spirit of the Fear of the LORD** — Holy reverence sustaining eternal alignment; sanctifying divine reverence; the balance of awe and obedience.

7. **The Spirit of Judgment and Burning** — refining divine holiness; the fire that finalises perfection.

These are not seven beings, but **seven flames of one Fire**, the Holy Spirit streaming through the Branch, manifesting the complete order of God's government. The first is the Source; the rest are His expressions. The Spirit of the LORD rests; the rest releases rule. This is the government of the Spirit; stable, righteous, unending.

Here, *glory deepens into governance*: wisdom is not mere intellect; it is the administration of the invisible Kingdom through perfect alignment with the Spirit of Rest.

3. Soulogy — The Formation of Divine Perception

The Branch's soul was **trained by the fear of the LORD**, not by natural sight or hearing.

> *"He shall not judge after the sight of His eyes, neither reprove after the hearing of His ears." — Isaiah 11:3 KJV*

His soul functioned as a **mirror of the Spirit**, reflecting God's heart without distortion. When wisdom and understanding unite, perception becomes prophetic, not reactionary. The soul becomes the *seat of righteous judgment*, discerning truth beyond appearance.

This is the pattern of every son of Zion: our emotions, desires, and discernment must submit to the resting Spirit, until the soul becomes a throne for divine justice.

4. Physiology — The Rod in His Hand

The "rod" also represents the **human vessel**, the body, as the instrument of divine execution. In Moses' hand, the rod parted seas; in Aaron's hand, it budded; in Christ's hand, it rules nations with righteousness.

> *"With righteousness shall He judge the poor,*
> *and reprove with equity for the meek of the*
> *earth: and He shall smite the earth with the*
> *rod of His mouth." — Isaiah 11:4 KJV*

The **mouth becomes the rod** — flesh carrying Word. The body becomes a temple; the tongue becomes a sceptre. Thus, the physiology of the Branch is prophetic: every organ serves the Spirit, every breath releases decree, and every action becomes worship that governs creation.

5. Theology — The Rebirth of the Davidic Covenant

Isaiah 11 is the **prophetic rebirth of 2 Samuel 7**; the covenant that promised David an everlasting throne. Christ, as the Rod from Jesse, is the embodiment of that eternal oath. His governance is not political but **pneumatic**; ruled by breath, Spirit, and righteousness.

David's songs became His decrees; His throne became Christ's cross. Out of suffering, wisdom was perfected; out of obedience, dominion was restored. The theology of this Branch is clear: **the kingdom of God advances through righteousness, not revolt**; through the inner Spirit of counsel, not carnal power.

6. Chronology — The Promise Preserved Through Exile

From Jesse to David, from David to exile, from exile to Christ; the timeline looked severed. But the Spirit hid the covenant inside **roots**, not branches. While branches can be cut, roots abide in darkness until light returns.

Chronologically, *Isaiah 11* bridges:

- **The fall of Judah (Tree cut)**

- **The exile (Root buried)**

- **The advent of Christ (Branch rising)**

- **The millennial reign (Rest established)**

Thus, every generation carries the *seed of the promise*, even in obscurity. What looks dead in time is alive in eternity.

7. Typology — David's Covenant Reborn through Wisdom

David received the pattern of divine rule through worship; Christ fulfilled it through wisdom and understanding.
David fought with his hands; Christ ruled with words.
David's harp restored the atmosphere; Christ's mouth restores order.

As David typifies the **heart of divine governance**, Christ manifests the **mind of divine wisdom**. Hence, in Him, worship becomes government, and wisdom becomes throne.

8. Technology — The Spiritual Architecture of Rest

The Spirit resting upon the Branch is not just an anointing but a **technology of habitation**. The sevenfold Spirits operate like chambers of divine intelligence; systems within the soul that align creation to heaven's rhythm.

Where the Spirit of Wisdom and Understanding reign, confusion dies, and governance flows. This is **the Sabbath technology of rule**: dominion without striving, victory without war, authority without rebellion. It is governance born from the peace of perfect understanding.

9. The Harmony of Creation — When Knowledge Covers the Earth

> *"For the earth shall be full of the knowledge of the*
> *LORD, as the waters cover the sea." — Isaiah 11:9 KJV*

The fruit of the Branch is **universal peace through spiritual illumination**. Knowledge (da'ath) here is not information but *union*. When the Spirit rests on man and man rests in Spirit, the whole earth reflects that communion.
Wolves dwell with lambs, leopards with kids; predatory nature is dissolved by divine wisdom.

This is the **prophetic ecology of Sabbath**, where all creation operates by harmony, not hostility.

10. Zionic Fulfilment — The Root Raised as a Standard

> *"In that day there shall be a root of Jesse, which shall*
> *stand for an ensign of the people." — Isaiah 11:10 KJV*

Christ, the Root, becomes the **Banner of Rest;** the standard of a new creation. His resurrection was not just a victory over death but the raising of the *Rod of Government.*

Those who gather under His ensign are sons of wisdom; the Branches of the Branch — trees of righteousness, oaks of understanding.

When the Spirit of Wisdom and Understanding rests upon the church, governance returns to Zion. Glory no longer visits; it dwells. The throne is not afar; it abides within.

Summary Revelation

The Rod from Jesse is the *resting place of the Spirit of Wisdom and Understanding.* Through Him, we learn that **true glory is not in exaltation but in habitation;** not in might but in mind, not in the noise of power but the silence of understanding.

The Sabbath rests in such men.
The Kingdom is safe in such minds.
And the Spirit finds home in such branches.

CHAPTER 9

The Branch of My Planting

"Thy people also shall be all righteous: they shall inherit the land for ever, the branch of My planting, the work of My hands, that I may be glorified." — Isaiah 60:21 (KJV)

Theme: The Planting of God — Where Dominion Becomes Inheritance

Theology — The Divine Gardener:

Planting is the act of incarnation; God descending into soil to produce sons. The Branch of His planting is not a work of man, but a revelation of God's inner nature expressed in human form. Adam was the first soil; Christ, the first Seed; the Spirit, the eternal Gardener. Where the Father plants, He intends to dwell. The planting of God is the habitation of God.

Righteousness is not achieved but **rooted**, established in the divine pattern of His own life.

Man becomes the garden where the Word takes flesh,

and every branch becomes the evidence of the invisible Hand.

Spiritology — The Planting as Infusion:

Planting in the Spirit is infusion, not addition.
The seed does not stand apart from the soil; it merges, transforms, and redefines it.
When God plants His Word within a vessel, the vessel becomes part of the vine's living system. The Spirit moves not above man, but through man; as sap through branch, as breath through lungs, as light through crystal.

Thus, "the work of My hands" means the divine pulse working inwardly; the same energy that raised Christ from the dead now rooting and branching in the believer's being.

The Spirit does not visit the branch — He becomes its circulation.

Soulogy — The Garden Within:

The human soul is the field of God. It has furrows; memories, affections, desires — where seeds are sown and storms are endured. Each revelation, each obedience, is a watering; each trial, a breaking of hard ground. When the soul yields, it becomes fertile; when it resists, it turns to stone.

To be "the branch of His planting" is to allow the Spirit to own the soil of your thoughts and emotions.
The soul no longer produces thorns of reasoning, but fruits of revelation.
Hope grows deep; peace shades the heart; joy blossoms as continual worship.

Physiology — The Human Vessel as Ground:

The body is not excluded from this planting.
The bones are stakes; the blood, divine irrigation; the breath, wind in the branches.

The Spirit's rooting transforms physiology; lungs become censers of prayer, hands become extensions of divine touch, eyes become gates of light.

The more the Spirit roots within, the more the mortal becomes fertile with immortality. This is not a metaphor; it is divine reality: the vessel becomes the vine's visible expression in the earth.

Typology — Trees of Righteousness:

Isaiah calls them *"trees of righteousness"* because righteousness is not an act; it's an ecosystem. Every tree reproduces after its kind; so the righteous reproduce righteousness. Their fruit is judgment; their leaves, healing; their root, covenant. Each tree becomes a testimony; planted not in Eden, but as Eden.

Christ, the True Vine, planted Himself in death so that many trees might live. His resurrection was not an escape from the ground, but fruit from within it.

Prophetic View — The Inheritance of the Branch:

When God says, "They shall inherit the land forever,"
He speaks of more than geography — He speaks of government. Land represents dominion; inheritance represents manifestation. The Branch of His planting will reign, not by force, but by fruit.

Zion becomes the mind renewed, Jerusalem becomes the heart inhabited, and the land becomes the body transformed, until every domain of man is saturated with divine presence.

Application — Becoming His Planting:

To be the Branch of His planting is to live as the Father's ecosystem on earth. Let the Word break your ground, let the

Spirit water your roots, let righteousness anchor your growth.

You are not a branch of ambition — you are the *Branch of His planting*. When He plants you, He glorifies Himself through your abiding. Every pruning is proof of His ownership, every fruit, a revelation of His nature.

For the planting of the LORD never withers, and every branch rooted in His Word shall live forever.

CHAPTER 10

The Righteous Branch and the
Throne of David of the Covenant

"Behold, the days come, saith the LORD, that I will
raise unto David a righteous Branch, and a King
shall reign and prosper, and shall execute judgment
and justice in the earth." — Jeremiah 23:5

"In those days, and at that time, will I cause the
Branch of righteousness to grow up unto David;
and he shall execute judgment and righteousness
in the land. In those days shall Judah be saved,
and Jerusalem shall dwell safely: and this is the
name wherewith she shall be called, THE LORD
OUR RIGHTEOUSNESS." — Jeremiah 33:15–16

Theme: The Planted Branch Becomes the Reigning King

Theology — The Covenant Root Grown into Reign:

E very covenant begins in promise and ends in government. The Branch of David was planted as Word, grew through obedience, and matured into a throne where righteousness and judgment dwell together (Psalm 97:2).

God did not raise a political dynasty but a *spiritual dominion*; a kingdom whose root is righteousness and whose fruit is judgment.

In Christ, the covenant of David becomes eternal because the throne is no longer made of gold but of Spirit; enthroned in Zion (the renewed mind) and Jerusalem (the purified heart).

Righteousness is not merely virtue; it is divine alignment; God reigning through a human will perfectly harmonised with His own.

Judgment is not destruction; it is divine order restoring balance to creation.

Thus, the Branch reigns not *over* the nations first, but *within* the sons who carry His nature.

Spiritology — The Branch as Spirit-Government:

When the Branch matures, the sap becomes law. This is the mystery of the Spirit's governance; the internalisation of divine command.

In the prophets, governance flowed from the temple; in the Christ, it flows from within.

The *Spirit of the LORD* — Identity and Dominion — channels into the sevenfold flow: Wisdom, Understanding, Counsel, Might, Knowledge, Fear of the LORD, and finally the Spirit of Judgment and Burning. These are not attributes beside the King; they are *His government in motion*.

The Branch reigns because the Spirit flows through every

chamber of His being, making Him both Priest and King, both Root and Crown.

When that same Spirit abides in man, the believer becomes a throne of righteousness; a living continuation of David's covenant.

Soulogy — The Inner Government of Zion and Jerusalem:

In every redeemed life, there are two thrones to reconcile:
Zion — the mind, where truth is seated;
Jerusalem — the heart, where love rules.

When these two unite, peace becomes law. Righteousness flows from Zion downward; mercy ascends from Jerusalem upward; and in their meeting place, the Spirit enthrones the King.

The soul that has both truth and love joined under one Spirit is no longer divided; it becomes a kingdom. Thought and affection obey the same King; obedience becomes joy; discernment becomes rest.

This is how inner government mirrors divine order. Judgment purifies thought — righteousness stabilises emotion; and together they manifest *shalom* — the wholeness of divine rule.

Physiology — The Body as Throne:

The throne of David now takes residence in the body of the believer. Every joint that yields to the Spirit becomes a gate of governance. The heart pulses divine justice; the hands enact divine will; the tongue decrees what heaven has written.

The King reigns from within flesh; not by the sword, but by the Word made living. The mortal becomes royal because the Branch of righteousness now extends through its veins. The throne of God and of the Lamb is no longer distant; it beats within redeemed blood.

Prophetic View — The Government of the Branch:

The Branch rising out of David is also the Vine that now carries us. In this hour, the Spirit extends His rule through those who abide in that Vine. Each yielded vessel becomes an embassy of Zion; a living decree of divine justice.

As it was spoken: *"Judah shall be saved, and Jerusalem shall dwell safely."*
Judah — praise — is salvation expressed; Jerusalem — peace — is habitation realised. When praise and peace coexist in the Spirit, the Kingdom stands unshakable.

And she — the corporate Bride — is called **THE LORD OUR RIGHTEOUSNESS**,
because her righteousness is not her own; it is His indwelling order ruling through her.

Application — Reigning from the Root:

To reign as a branch is not to ascend in pride but to deepen in obedience. The throne of God is reached not by climbing but by yielding. He raises only what has surrendered to His planting.

Let the Word take root in your thought;
let the Spirit prune your emotions;
let righteousness become your law and judgment your discernment. Then the King reigns not only *for* you but *through* you.

Zion in your mind shall decree, Jerusalem in your heart shall manifest, and together they shall say, **"The LORD reigneth; the earth is full of His glory."**

CHAPTER 11

The Servant and the Builder
(Zechariah 3:8; 6:12–13)

"Behold the man whose name is The Branch; and he shall grow up out of his place, and he shall build the temple of the LORD… even he shall build the temple of the LORD; and he shall bear the glory, and shall sit and rule upon his throne; and he shall be a priest upon his throne: and the counsel of peace shall be between them both." — Zechariah 6:12–13 (KJV)

Theme: The Priest-King Who Builds by the Spirit and Word

The Dual Mantle of the Branch

In the prophetic lens of Zechariah, The Branch appears not merely as a figure of restoration but as the fusion of two eternal offices; priesthood and kingship. He is the Servant of obedience and the Builder of dominion.

Where the priest reconciles God and man, the king governs what has been reconciled.

In Christ — the Man called The Branch; these two streams converge into one river of peace: the counsel of heaven and earth in perfect agreement.

The priest ministers upward; the king administers outward. The Branch stands between both, embodying the architecture of reconciliation.

Theology — Christ the Divine Architect

The phrase *"He shall build the temple of the LORD"* reveals not carpentry but divine architecture. Christ builds not with stones, but with **spirits quickened by His Word.** He is the Living Blueprint, the eternal pattern after which all creation aligns (*Hebrews 8:5; John 1:3*).

When He said, *"Upon this rock I will build My Church,"* (**Matthew 16:18**), He spoke not of mortar and pillars but of the revelation of Himself; the Word incarnate, constructing a spiritual house whose foundation is truth.

The **theology of the Builder** is therefore this: Every true temple must be built by the Word and governed by the Spirit. All else collapses under the weight of time.

In the heavens, the pattern was fire; on the earth, it becomes flesh. Thus, *The Branch* carries within Himself the very form of divine construction; the mind, heart, and body aligned as God's sanctuary.

Spiritology — Building by Breath and Fire

The Spirit of the LORD is the living Architect's breath.
Every measure, dimension, and ornament of God's temple originates from His sevenfold Spirit:

- Spirit of Wisdom — designs the unseen framework.

- Spirit of Understanding — interprets divine proportion.

- Spirit of Counsel — guides every joint and corner.

- Spirit of Might — establishes strength to bear glory.

- Spirit of Knowledge — orders the laws of function.

- Spirit of the Fear of the LORD — consecrates the foundation.

- Spirit of Judgment and Burning — seals the house with fire.

This is how the Branch builds; not through human power or political vision, but through the inner blueprint breathed by the Spirit. Each believer becomes a **living stone**, each obedience a **measured cubit**, and each prayer a **beam of light** supporting the eternal structure of God's habitation.

Soulogy — The Inner Construction of the Temple

The soul itself must be built before the city can be restored. Zechariah's vision of Joshua the high priest (**Zechariah 3**) is not a ceremony in heaven, but a blueprint of inner transformation. The filthy garments are stripped; the pure mitre is placed; this is the **renovation of the inner man.**

In soulogy, *building the temple* means aligning thought, will, and emotion under divine government. Each part of the soul becomes a chamber of worship when surrendered to the Spirit. The mind becomes the Holy Place of revelation; the heart becomes the Altar of Incense; and the body becomes the Outer Court where obedience is manifested.

Thus, every righteous man is not only a branch but a *builder* of his own inner temple.

Physiology — The Body as the Living Architecture of God

Paul declared, *"Know ye not that your body is the temple of the Holy Ghost?"* (**1 Corinthians 6:19**). Physiologically, the human frame mirrors the tabernacle. The **sevenfold lampstand** aligns with the **seven vital systems** of life; the **altar of sacrifice** with the **heart** that circulates blood and fire; and the **veil** with the human mind, where revelation must tear before Spirit and soul unite.

When The Branch builds, He engraves His law into this body-temple; nerve by nerve, breath by breath. Hence, redemption is architectural; salvation is structural; it is the rebuilding of the fallen tabernacle of Adam into the living body of Christ.

Chronology — From Zerubbabel to Christ the Cornerstone

Historically, Zechariah spoke to a generation rebuilding physical ruins under **Zerubbabel**, yet prophetically, the message pointed to Christ, the true Zerubbabel, whose name means *"Born in Babylon."* He would arise from the ruin of human failure to finish the temple that no man could complete.

> *"Not by might, nor by power, but by My Spirit, saith the LORD of hosts." — Zechariah 4:6*

The same voice that laid the foundation now cries from Zion, *"Grace, grace unto it!"* Chronologically, every rebuilding — from Solomon to Ezra to Nehemiah — foreshadowed this ultimate construction: a **temple not made with hands**, wherein God Himself would dwell eternally.

Typology — The Crowned Priest-King

The crown of *Zechariah 6:11* unites priesthood and kingship; two offices once separated by law, now fused in grace. Melchizedek foreshadowed this union: "King of righteousness" and "priest of the Most High God." The Branch fulfills that type, wearing both mitre and crown "Holiness unto the LORD under the power of Christ".

In Him, the altar and the throne meet. He rules from within the place of sacrifice. Thus, true governance is born from worship, and true worship flows from authority.

Every believer who abides in this Branch carries that dual mantle: priestly intercession and kingly dominion.

Technology — Building by the Word and Spirit

The "technology" of divine construction is **spiritual sound and sacred design.** When God speaks, creation takes form; when man echoes that Word in faith, the invisible becomes visible.

Christ builds by the **frequency of truth;** His voice is the template, and His Spirit the energy of completion. In this prophetic dimension, "technology" refers not to machines but to the laws by which God engineers existence.

- The **Word** is the blueprint (Logos).

- The **Spirit** is the power (Pneuma).

- The **Voice of Faith** is the tool (Rhema).

The Servant and Builder operates by aligning these three: Word, Spirit, and Speech, until heaven's plan becomes earth's manifestation. Hence, the temple of the last days is being raised not by hands, but by prophetic decree and obedience to revelation.

Prophetic View — The Final Builder Generation

The Branch has many branches; a remnant generation anointed with the same dual mantle: to serve as priests and to build as kings. This generation does not construct cathedrals but **habitations of righteousness**; not altars of stone, but **altars of hearts.**

They restore worship as architecture, governance as service, and truth as foundation. Through them, the earth becomes the Lord's temple again; the mountain of His house is established above all hills (*Isaiah 2:2*).

Their anthem is Zechariah's word reborn:

> *"Behold the Man whose name is The Branch... He shall build the temple of the LORD, and He shall bear the glory."*

Prophetic Conclusion — The Counsel of Peace Between Them Both

When priest and king unite, the counsel of peace is established. In Christ, heaven and earth reconcile; in His body, Word and Spirit agree. This is the mystery of the Servant and Builder; that God would not only dwell with man but *within* man, and that the same hands once pierced by nails now construct the eternal dwelling of glory.

The Branch builds the temple of the LORD, and the temple He builds is *you.*

PART IV — THE CUT AND THE PLANTING

THE BRANCH IN JUDGMENT AND RESTORATION (Ezekiel–Daniel–Malachi)

CHAPTER 12

*The Highest Branch in
Judgment and Restoration
(Isaiah 14–Ezekiel 17)*

*Where the counterfeit branches are judged and the
true Branch is exalted on the holy mountain of Zion.*

The Eagle and the Cedar — The Parable of Dominion

Ezekiel's vision reveals two eagles and a cedar; a mystery of governments and glories. The first eagle represents the proud dominion of fallen principalities who pluck the highest branches and plant them in foreign soil (*Ezekiel 17:3–4*). These are the powers that exalted themselves above the stars of God (*Isaiah 14:13*), the proud roots of Babylon and Luciferic dominion. But the second eagle — the covenantal image of the LORD Himself — returns to plant **a tender twig from the highest branch** upon a **high and eminent mountain** (*Ezekiel 17:22*). This is Christ, the humble Branch, planted in Zion to restore what was cut down by pride.

Theology — God the Planter and Judge

In the great controversy of gardens, the LORD proves Himself the only true Husbandman. Every branch not planted by His hand must be uprooted (*Matthew 15:13*).

The axe laid to the root (*Matthew 3:10*) is both judgment and mercy; the removal of false dominion so that divine order can be reestablished.

God's judgment is not destruction; it is divine horticulture. He prunes the nations so that His righteous Branch may spread again upon the mountains of Israel.

Spiritology — Humility: The Root of Exaltation

The tender branch is the mystery of meekness enthroned. Where Lucifer sought to ascend through pride, Christ descended through humility, and was exalted far above all heavens (*Philippians 2:8–9*). The Spirit of the Branch is the Spirit of lowliness that receives high places.

For in the laws of divine life, **the lowest root carries the highest fruit**.

Humility is not weakness; it is divine gravity. It pulls glory downward so that grace may grow upward.

Soulogy — The Fall of False Branches

The soul that exalts itself in self-righteousness or knowledge without submission becomes like a cedar planted in strange waters; green for a time, but with no covenantal root. The lofty branches of pride are cut down in judgment so that the soul may return to stillness before God.

When man's reasoning, ambition, or self-will climbs above his obedience, it becomes a false branch, and must wither.

In the pruning of the soul, false branches fall so that the sap of truth may flow freely once more.

Physiology — The Mountain of the Body

The "high mountain of Israel" also symbolises the sanctified body; the temple restored for the indwelling Spirit.

Where once serpents ruled the dust, now the Branch of Life rises within the human form as the Tree of the LORD.

When the Spirit plants the tender twig within the heart, the body becomes Zion, the mountain where divine life takes root in flesh. The restoration of the branch is therefore not external but internal; the Spirit reclaims His sanctuary within man.

Typology — From Nebuchadnezzar to Messiah

Ezekiel's parable finds fulfilment in both judgment and promise. The fall of Babylon's cedar (*Isaiah 14*) typifies the downfall of the proud, while the planting of the tender branch foreshadows the reign of Messiah.

The tree imagery in Daniel and Ezekiel are one; Nebuchadnezzar's tree was cut down, but Christ's tree was raised up. Thus, history bends around a single prophecy: **the high made low, and the low exalted.**

Chronology — Restoration in the Last Days

We live in the era of the tender twig's manifestation; the final planting before the consummation of ages. The LORD is exalting His holy mountain — the true Zion — and the remnant Branch is growing into a global cedar of righteousness.

Every false system, empire, and ecclesiastical tree that stood in pride will be cut down before this planting. For it is written, *"All the trees of the field shall know that I the LORD have brought down the high tree, have exalted the low tree, have dried up the green tree, and have made the dry tree to flourish"* (*Ezekiel 17:24*).

The Prophetic Conclusion — The Mountain of the Branch

The culmination of the Branch mystery is this: The government of the heavens will be rooted in the humility of Zion. Christ — the tender twig; will stretch forth His branches across nations, and every people will find shelter in His shadow. And from that high and holy mountain will flow the River of Life, watering the roots of every righteous soul that abides in Him.

CHAPTER 13

The Branch in the Fire
(Ezekiel 15; Malachi 4:1)

Where judgment becomes purification, and fire reveals the true nature of every branch.

The Parable of the Vine — Uselessness without Fruit

Ezekiel's vision of the vine declares a sobering truth: a branch without fruit cannot be used for building, only for burning. The vine, when detached from the root, loses its divine purpose; for its strength lies not in its wood but in its fruit.

God asks, *"Shall wood be taken thereof to do any work?"* (**Ezekiel 15:3**). The answer is no. It is good only to be cast into the fire. Thus, the fire that consumes is not arbitrary destruction; it is divine exposure. The fruitless branch faces flame because it no longer reflects the life of the Vine. In every age, God tries His people by fire to reveal whether their connection to Him is living or merely religious.

Theology — Fire as Divine Justice and Renewal

Fire is not merely punishment; it is the nature of God's holiness in motion. For our God is a consuming fire (*Deuteronomy 4:24; Hebrews 12:29*). When the fire of God touches a thing, it either refines it or removes it.

In theology, this fire is covenantal; it preserves the righteous and destroys the counterfeit. The same flame that burned Sodom also filled the upper room. It purges the dross, but it never harms gold. Therefore, the fire that falls on the Branch is not to destroy it but to unveil its incorruptible core; the righteousness of Christ within.

Spiritology — The Fire of Purification

The fire operates in three dimensions:

- **Consuming Fire** — judgment against rebellion.
- **Refining Fire** — purification of the faithful.
- **Revealing Fire** — manifestation of hidden glory.

When the Spirit baptizes with fire (*Matthew 3:11*), He ignites within the believer the process of divine calibration. Every false motive, pride, and impurity is tested by this internal flame until what remains is pure light.

The Spirit of Burning (*Isaiah 4:4*) is therefore the sanctifier of the Branch. It burns not to wound but to renew; for resurrection life is born only from ashes.

Soulogy — The Inner Furnace

In the soul, the fire represents the trials that confront the will, emotions, and intellect. When faith is tested, the soul becomes the altar, and endurance the sacrifice. Every true branch must pass through this inward furnace where trust in God replaces self-preservation.

The righteous man does not escape fire; he is *refined* by it.

Just as gold cannot boast until it has endured the flame, the soul cannot mirror Christ until it has walked through affliction. The furnace is the classroom of faith where the Word becomes experience and knowledge becomes intimacy.

Physiology — Fire and the Body as a Living Altar

The body itself becomes a vessel of transformation. When the Spirit's fire moves through the physical form, it quickens every cell, consumes corruption, and awakens holiness. Paul wrote, *"Present your bodies a living sacrifice, holy, acceptable unto God"* (**Romans 12:1**). This is the physiology of fire; the offering of the flesh until the Spirit governs completely.

In such purification, sicknesses, lusts, and addictions are burned away; not by human striving but by divine flame.
The body of the righteous man becomes the temple-fire where the Spirit dwells continually.

Typology — The Fiery Law and the Branch of Truth

In typology, the fire is the *Law of God in manifestation.*
When Moses received the commandments, they were delivered "from His right hand went a fiery law" (**Deuteronomy 33:2**). That same fiery Word now operates through the Branch, refining every son whom God receives (**Hebrews 12:6**).

The fruitless branch symbolises Israel's rebellion, yet through Christ — the true Vine — the fire becomes redemptive. The burning of the old gives way to the blossoming of the new. In Him, judgment and mercy meet; for the branch that abides in the Vine cannot be consumed; it only glows.

Chronology — From Babylon's Fire to the Day of the LORD

Historically, Ezekiel's prophecy prefigured the Babylonian captivity; a fire that purified Israel's remnant. But prophetically,

Malachi extends the flame to the final generation:

> *"Behold, the day cometh, that shall burn as*
> *an oven... but unto you that fear My name*
> *shall the Sun of righteousness arise with*
> *healing in His wings." (Malachi 4:1–2).*

This twofold day — burning and healing — defines the end-time baptism. The same flame that consumes the wicked will transfigure the righteous into glory. It is both judgment upon nations and illumination upon Zion.

Prophetic View — The Fire Within the Remnant

In the last days, the remnant will not fear the fire; they will *carry* it. The righteous shall shine as burning lamps before the throne (*Matthew 5:14; Revelation 4:5*). Their inner man will burn with the same flame that once filled the bush of Moses; aflame but not consumed.

This is the final identity of the Branch: not merely planted or flourishing, but *fiery.* It is the branch that has passed through the furnace and come forth as the likeness of the Son of Man; glowing with divine light, bearing the fire of eternal righteousness.

Prophetic Conclusion — From Burning to Shining

The Branch in the Fire is the transformation of judgment into radiance. It is where holiness overtakes fear, and death is swallowed by flame. For the branch that endures the fire becomes the lampstand of the Spirit; rooted in earth but burning with heaven.

As it is written:

"I the LORD have kindled it; it shall not be quenched." (Ezekiel 20:47)
And again,
"He shall baptize you with the Holy Ghost, and with fire." (Matthew 3:11)

CHAPTER 14

The Branch of Her Roots
(Daniel 11:7)

"But out of a branch of her roots shall one stand up in his estate, which shall come with an army, and shall enter into the fortress of the king of the north..." — Daniel 11:7 (KJV)

Theme: The Hidden Root Rising Through Conflict

The Hidden Continuation

History bends toward covenant. Even in exile, the bloodline of promise does not end — it hides. When empires rise and crumble, a remnant root keeps breathing under the dust. Daniel foresaw this: out of affliction's ground, a branch of her roots would stand again; a figure of both resistance and redemption.

In every generation, God plants continuity beneath collapse.

Chronology — The Covenant Thread Through War and Empire

Daniel's vision traces the political convulsions between the North and South, but behind the battles moves a quieter story: *the preservation of divine lineage.* When kingdoms clash, heaven guards the seed. Empires shift, but inheritance remains buried, waiting for the appointed season.

This "branch of her roots" arises not as a conqueror of nations but as a testimony of endurance. From Abraham to David, from Judah to the exiles, the same covenant breathes beneath the ashes. Even when kings forget Zion, heaven remembers the root.

Every collapse of empire is a pruning; every remnant that survives is a root finding air again.

Theology — Covenant in Continuity

God never begins again — He restores. The root carries the record of divine promise, and every new branch grows from what was once cut down. That is covenant: not repetition, but resurrection. He said to Israel, *"I will not make a full end."*

The **branch of her roots** is the mystery of divine mercy; that judgment never severs grace, it only refines its vessel. When the axe falls, God hides the seed. The branch rises again when the season of testing is complete.

Spiritology — The Law of Hidden Growth

Spiritually, roots represent the unseen obedience of faith.
They absorb in silence, unseen by men but known by heaven. When a branch emerges from its roots after great affliction, it testifies that hidden faith never dies. It is the *law of continuity* in the Spirit, that what God plants cannot perish, only transform.

So the "branch of her roots" is the inner man reborn from buried faith. Affliction drove the righteous underground, but it also purified their sap. The Spirit refines the root so that when it emerges, it bears fruit untainted by the soil of corruption.

Soulogy — The Ancestry of the Inner Life

Every soul carries ancestry, memory, covenant, and test. Daniel's prophecy mirrors an inner drama: the faithful part of the soul rising from the ruins of broken identity. Out of what was wounded, God raises a new strength; not foreign to the old, but born from its purified core.

Thus, in the soul, the *branch of her roots* is the reawakening of divine remembrance. The Spirit digs deep, past the mind's ruins, to awaken what He once planted before birth; the seed of covenant identity.

Typology — The Woman, the Root, and the Remnant

The "her" in *"branch of her roots"* speaks prophetically of Zion, the covenant mother, whose roots lie in God's promise. Though her sons were scattered and her land desolate, out of her the Branch rises again. This echoes *Isaiah 11:1*: *"A rod out of the stem of Jesse."* Each image points to the same pattern — **the feminine root (Zion)** conceiving again through **the Spirit of promise.**

Typologically, it also points to the Church; a remnant womb that carries resurrection in its roots. From the ashes of compromise, God raises a purified witness, untouched by the corruption of empire.

Prophetic View — The Rising of the Root Generation

The final generation is not a new creation apart from history; it is the *branch of her roots* — a continuation of the ancient covenant line now perfected in Spirit. They arise in the estate of fallen thrones, carrying not weapons of war but *the Word of restoration.* Their victory is not territorial but spiritual: They overthrow lies with truth, rebuild altars in ruined nations, and awaken the memory of Zion within man.

This generation will know where they came from, and in that remembrance, they will find authority. The Spirit of the LORD will root them deep in covenant identity, and their fruit will endure when kingdoms fall again.

Application — Becoming the Branch of Continuity

To be a *branch of her roots* is to let God continue His story through you. It is to live as the unseen proof that His Word outlasts empire. It requires patience under pruning, faith under obscurity, and loyalty to the unseen lineage of light.

You are not a replacement — you are a continuation. The Spirit does not discard what is old; He sanctifies it. When He calls you a branch of the roots, He invites you to carry forward the memory of the covenant until it becomes glory again.

PART V — THE LIVING VINE

*THE BRANCH MANIFESTED
IN CHRIST (Gospels)*

Theme: The Fulfillment of the Pattern

CHAPTER 15

*The Parable of the Fig Tree
(Matthew 24:32–33; Mark
13:28–29; Luke 21:29–31)*

*"Now learn a parable of the fig tree; When his
branch is yet tender, and putteth forth leaves, ye
know that summer is nigh: So likewise ye, when ye
shall see all these things, know that it is near, even
at the doors." — Matthew 24:32–33 (KJV)*

The Parable as a Prophetic Cipher

When Christ spoke of the fig tree, He revealed not agriculture, but the anatomy of redemption; the awakening of the human spirit through the cycles of divine time.

From Genesis to Revelation, the fig tree represents the spirit of man that bears God's covenant identity — Israel, the "prince who prevails with God."

- Adam's fig leaves (*Genesis 3:7*) were the soul's attempt to hide the spirit's fall.

- The cursed fig tree (*Mark 11:13–14*) was judgment against religion that bears no spiritual fruit.

- The tender fig branch (*Matthew 24:32*) is the **reborn spirit of man** — restored, receptive, and ready for divine indwelling.

Thus, the parable encodes the *entire journey of the spirit* — from death in Adam to life in Christ.

Spiritology — The Spirit's Seasons of Awakening

The "tender branch" represents the **softened, regenerated human spirit**. It is the moment the inner man turns from hardness to tenderness, from religion to relationship, from law to life.

> *"A new heart also will I give you, and a new spirit will I put within you." — Ezekiel 36:26*

In this parable, Christ unveils the **seasonal clock of the spirit**:

Spiritual Season	Condition of the Human Spirit	Dispensation
Winter	Spirit in darkness and dormancy (spiritual death)	The Fall and Dispersion
Spring	Spirit quickened by divine Word (rebirth begins)	The Coming of Christ
Summer	Spirit matured and fruitful (Sabbath	Millennial Reign and Glory

	Rest)	
Autumn	Spirit's fruit gathered in judgment	The Eternal Kingdom

When Jesus said, *"When ye see the branch tender,"* He spoke of the **rebirth of the human spirit**; the *Israel within man* awakening to the indwelling Spirit of Truth. Tenderness means **spiritual receptivity**; the ability of the spirit to once again respond to God's breath.

Soulogy — The Leaves of Self-Covering

Adam's use of fig leaves revealed the soul's impulse to cover what only the Spirit can restore. The **soul without Spirit** weaves coverings of self-effort, religion, and intellect — outward righteousness without inward life. Every system built by the soul apart from the Spirit becomes a "leafy tree without fruit."

When Christ cursed the barren fig tree, He was **condemning soulish religion** that looks alive but carries no Spirit. He judged the system that covers the spirit's nakedness instead of healing it.

In the reborn fig tree of *Matthew 24*, however, the **spirit is restored**; the leaves are no longer coverings of shame but **expressions of life**. The soul becomes the canopy of a Spirit-rooted man — redeemed, not self-made.

Physiology — The Vine and Circulation of Life

The fig tree and vine imagery both reveal the physiology of divine life.
Christ said:

"I am the Vine, ye are the branches." —John 15:5

The vine is Christ's Spirit; the branches are the spirits of men joined to Him. The **sap** is the Holy Ghost; the breath of God circulating through the collective Body.

When the branch is tender, it signifies that the **channels of life are open**; that the human spirit is no longer blocked by sin, pride, or hardness. Divine circulation has resumed. This tenderness is the restoration of Sabbath rest *within the body of man.*

The barren branch — religion without Spirit — is cut off.
The tender branch — Spirit-filled and submissive — abides and bears fruit.

Thus, the physiological parable points to a **body filled with the living Spirit**, functioning as one organism of divine flow — the Church of the Firstborn, the Vine of Zion.

Theology — Israel as the Spirit of Covenant

Israel is not the soul of humanity; Israel is the **spirit of covenant identity within humanity**. It is the divine spark placed in man that knows its Source and carries His Name.
The fig tree, therefore, symbolises **the reawakening of that covenant spirit;** the rebirth of divine identity in mankind.

- The *root* is Abrahamic faith (the covenant spirit).

- The *vine* is Christ (the Spirit made flesh).

- The *branch* is the reborn human spirit (sons of God).

- The *fruit* is righteousness and dominion (Spirit authority).

When the fig tree becomes tender, it means the **Spirit of Israel in man** is stirring again; the sons of God are remembering who they are. It is the signal that the **Sabbath age** — the 7th Day — is near, when Spirit will again govern flesh.

Typology — The Restoration Pattern

Symbol	Prophetic Type	Fulfilment
Fig Tree	The human spirit (Israel)	Restored to divine sensitivity
Tender Branch	Rebirth / Regeneration	Spirit quickened by the Word
Leaves	Knowledge, gifts, expressions	Outer signs of inner life
Fruit	Judgment, righteousness, glory	Mature sons manifesting Spirit nature
Summer	Sabbath fullness	The reign of the Spirit on earth

This typology shows that Christ's parable is not mere eschatology but **Spirit chronology;** the unfolding of divine life within humanity's spirit.

Prophetic Application — The Branch Man Restored

The "Branch Man" is the ultimate fulfilment of the fig tree parable. He is Christ multiplied; the Spirit of the Son reproduced in sons and daughters who walk as *living vines of light.* Their tenderness is obedience; their fruit is divine judgment and peace. They carry no fig leaves; no false coverings, for the Spirit Himself clothes them in glory.

As this Branch generation awakens, the clock of redemption moves toward the Sabbath hour. The parable is fulfilled not merely in Israel's land, but in *Israel's spirit*; the spirit of man reborn, indwelt, and governed by the Holy Ghost.

"When ye see these things… know that it is near."
Near — not destruction, but **indwelling.**
Near — not ending, but **enthronement.**
Near — the Spirit resting fully in man.

Key Revelations

1. The fig tree represents the **human spirit (Israel)** — the divine root within man.

2. The tender branch is the **rebirth and sensitivity of that spirit** to the Word.

3. The leaves symbolise **soulish expression** when the spirit governs rightly.

4. The fruit is **righteous dominion** — the manifestation of Spirit nature.

5. The summer season marks **the approach of Sabbath Rest —** Spirit reigning over soul and body.

6. The parable therefore, unveils the final awakening: *the Spirit of Israel restored in the sons of God.*

CHAPTER 16

The True Vine and The Branches
(John 15:1–8)

"I am the true vine, and my Father is the husbandman. Every branch in me that beareth not fruit he taketh away: and every branch that beareth fruit, he purgeth it, that it may bring forth more fruit." —John 15:1-2 (KJV)

Theme: The Law of Abiding — Divine Circulation of the Spirit Through the Body

In this revelation, Christ unveils the physiology of divine union: a living system where God, the Word, and man share one continuous circulation of Spirit. The Vine is Christ — not a tree of knowledge, but a Tree of Life restored. The Branches are not external extensions, but internal continuations of the Vine's essence; each a vessel through which the Spirit of the Word flows and bears fruit. Here, the mystery of all covenants is fulfilled: **God indwelling man**.

The branch no longer strives; it abides.

The soul no longer labours; it receives.

The spirit no longer wanders; it returns to its Source.

Theology — The Vine as the Incarnate Covenant

The Vine is Christ — the eternal Word made flesh, in whom all covenants converge. He is called "True Vine" because He restores what the **first vine (Adam)** corrupted. Adam's vine was self-knowledge; Christ's vine is divine nature. The first drew life from the earth; the second draws life from heaven.

The Father is the **Husbandman**; the eternal Gardener who plants, prunes, and perfects every branch according to the pattern of His will. He does not prune to destroy but to **increase divine capacity**. Every cut is an invitation to bear more Spirit.

This divine ecosystem is **covenantal**:

- The Vine carries the sap of the Spirit (the blood of divine life).

- The Branch receives that life by abiding.

- The Fruit manifests that life in tangible form — love, truth, and righteousness.

Thus, the Church is not an organisation but an **organism**; a single body, a vine of light, flowing with the same divine sap.

Spiritology — Abiding in the Word as Life

Christ said, *"Abide in Me, and I in you."* This is not a command of effort but a revelation of **indwelling identity**. The Word is not merely instruction; it is **breath**, **circulation**, and **communion**. To abide in the Word is to dwell in the current of the Spirit; the rhythm of divine respiration between heaven and man.

Abiding is the **Sabbath state of the spirit**: resting while producing, yielding while ruling. It is the law of stillness that governs all fruitfulness.

The Spirit of Truth is the sap that moves through the Vine. He connects every branch to the source of divine consciousness; the mind of Christ. Where the Spirit flows freely, revelation blossoms naturally. Fruit is never forced; it emerges as the overflow of abiding.

To abide is therefore to **remain aligned**:

- In Spirit — communion

- In Word — continuity

- In Obedience — channel

- In Love — circulation

This is the secret of divine life: **Spirit flows where the Word abides.**

Soulogy — Purging Through Truth

The soul is the vineyard's trellis; the framework that must be continually aligned to the Spirit's growth. Christ said, *"Ye are clean through the word which I have spoken unto you."* (**John 15:3**) This cleansing is the **purging process**; the pruning of the soul by truth.

Every thought, desire, and emotion that does not carry the sap of the Spirit must be pruned. Pruning feels like loss, but it is **the Spirit's surgery for expansion**. Truth cuts the unnecessary so that love can fill the void.

Soulish religion resists pruning; it clings to leaves (appearances) instead of fruit (righteousness). But the abiding soul welcomes the knife of truth, knowing that **pruning is proof of connection**. If you are being purified, it means you are still alive in the Vine.

The purpose of purging is not to punish but to **prepare for deeper indwelling**. The purged soul becomes translucent; no longer obstructing the Spirit's light but transmitting it freely.

Physiology — Divine Circulation: The Flow of Spirit Through the Body

The Vine and Branches reveal **the physiology of Christ's Body**. Just as the human body carries blood, the spiritual body carries **Spirit**. The Holy Ghost is the **circulatory system of divinity,** connecting every member to the heart of Christ.

When the branch abides, the sap flows.
When the branch disconnects, stagnation sets in.
Sin is not merely moral failure; it is **spiritual disconnection**, the interruption of divine flow.

In this physiology:

- The **Vine** is the spinal column — the Word incarnate.

- The **Branches** are the nerves and limbs — expressions of divine life.

- The **Fruit** is the visible evidence of inner flow — righteousness, peace, and joy in the Holy Ghost.

Thus, the Church — the collective body of believers — is not a mechanical structure but **a living vine of divine physiology**, circulating one Spirit through many vessels.

Wherever circulation ceases, pruning restores it. Wherever it flows, the light of divine health and holiness emerges.

Typology — From Israel's Vine to the True Vine

Israel was called "a noble vine" (*Jeremiah 2:21*), but it degenerated through self-dependence. Its fruit became ritual instead of righteousness. Christ came as the **True Vine** — the fulfilment of what Israel was meant to be:
a nation of spirits fully rooted in God.

In typology:

- The **wild vine** represents corrupted religion and self-rule.

- The **true vine** represents divine nature restored through the Spirit.

- The **branches** represent regenerated human spirits.

- The **fruit** represents manifest sonship — the outward evidence of inward Spirit-life.

Through this typology, Christ replaces the old national vine with a **universal spiritual vine**; a kingdom of priests, a people of Spirit, bearing fruit across every nation and tongue.

Chronology — The Vine Through the Ages

1. **In Eden:** The vine of self — knowledge without obedience.

2. **In Israel:** The vine of the covenant — shadow without substance.

3. **In Christ:** The true vine — Spirit and truth united.

4. **In the Church:** The vine multiplied — many branches, one Spirit.

5. **In Zion:** The vine enthroned — the Bride and the Spirit as one tree of life.

Thus, *John 15* is not the beginning but the culmination of all vine imagery: **the restoration of the Tree of Life in the hearts of men**.

Prophetic Application — The Law of Abiding

To abide is to **cease from struggle** and **enter into divine rhythm**. It is to let the Word think, feel, and act through you. You no longer "serve" the Vine; you **become one with its flow**.

Fruit-bearing is no longer a task but a *state of being*.

- The abiding spirit walks in perpetual communion.

- The abiding soul rests under continual pruning.

- The abiding body becomes a vessel of divine health and holiness.

Every breath becomes worship; every silence, intercession. Such a life fulfils the mystery: *"Christ in you, the hope of glory."*

The Sabbath of Abiding — Rest as Dominion

When a branch abides perfectly, it no longer struggles to live; it simply **remains connected**. That is the Sabbath state. In the Vine, work becomes worship; fruit becomes identity. The flow of Spirit replaces the labour of the flesh. This is the eternal order of divine rest; **not inactivity, but unbroken circulation.**

*"He that abideth in Me, and I in him, the
same bringeth forth much fruit: for without
Me ye can do nothing." —John 15:5*

Abiding is not passivity; it is perfect participation in divine motion — **the stillness that rules creation.**

Key Revelations

1. The Vine is Christ — the Spirit-Word incarnate.

2. The Branch is the reborn human spirit — the vessel of divine life.

3. The Sap is the Holy Ghost — the circulation of divine consciousness.

4. The Husbandman is the Father — pruning to perfect flow.

5. The Fruit is righteousness and dominion — evidence of

inner life.

6. Abiding is the law of Sabbath — divine rest in motion.

7. Purging is proof of love — every wound is a window for more Spirit.

Prophetic Declaration

"I am a living branch in the Vine of Light.
The Word flows through me as breath, fire, and wisdom.
The Father's pruning does not harm but enlarges me.
Every cut becomes a channel of glory.
I abide, and therefore I reign.
For without Him, I am nothing;
but in Him, I am all that He is."

PART VI — THE RIGHTEOUS BRANCH MULTIPLIED

THE SONS OF ZION
(Acts–Revelation)

CHAPTER 17

The Outpouring Branch (Acts 2)

"And there appeared unto them cloven tongues like as of fire, and it sat upon each of them. And they were all filled with the Holy Ghost, and began to speak with other tongues, as the Spirit gave them utterance." — Acts 2:3–4 (KJV)

Theme: The Branch Becomes Many — Fire Divided Yet One

Pentecost was not the birth of a new faith but the unveiling of a living Body. The single Vine of Christ blossomed into many branches of flame, each one carrying the same sap of the Spirit. The fire that once rested upon the candlestick now sat upon human heads. The temple had shifted from building to being.

The cloven tongues were not chaos; they were **multiplication of one language into many frequencies of Spirit**.

It was God speaking Himself through man, not man learning to speak like God. The Word had found new bodies. The Branch had become a Body.

Theology — The Covenant Transferred from Temple to Body

The Spirit did not descend on stones, but on spirits. This marked the final fulfilment of the prophecy:

"I will pour out My Spirit upon all flesh." —Joel 2:28

The old temple system ended where the new temple began — **in living branches**. Christ, the True Vine, had completed His earthly work; now the Spirit extended His life into every believer. The covenant was no longer written on tablets but **encoded in breath**. The law that once carved commandments now carved **consciousness**.

The Father, the Husbandman, no longer walked in a garden but **dwelt within the vine itself**. Every branch became an altar; every breath, an offering.

This is the theology of Pentecost: **God multiplied Himself through His Body.**

Spiritology — The Fire of Communion

Cloven tongues of fire rested upon them; not to burn, but to **bond**. Each flame was a mirror of the same Spirit, divided but not separated. Just as the seven lamps of fire before the throne are one Spirit in seven expressions (**Revelation 4:5**), so the tongues of fire were **many expressions of one flame**.

The Spirit of the LORD — the Holy Spirit Himself — streamed through His sevenfold rivers:

- Wisdom speaking through revelation,

- Understanding through interpretation,

- Counsel through utterance,

- Might through authority,

- Knowledge through intimacy,

- Fear through holiness,

- Judgment and Burning through purification.

Every tongue was a **branch of the same fire**, every word, a **pulse of divine light**.

This was not emotional expression; it was **spiritual communication**, the rebirth of Edenic speech — Word flowing directly from Spirit. The human mouth became the gate of divine utterance. Language was redeemed as the first instrument of dominion. God speaking with stammering lips with another tongue to his people.

Soulogy — Transformation Through Speech

Speech reveals the soul. Before Pentecost, the disciples spoke from fear and doubt. After Pentecost, they spoke from union. Their tongues were no longer servants of confusion but instruments of Spirit.

When the Spirit fills the soul, speech is sanctified. The mind stops processing words — it starts *translating fire*.
This is the reversal of Babel. At Babel, one language was divided to scatter men. At Pentecost, one Spirit spoke in many tongues to unite men.

True unity is not sameness of language, but **oneness of Spirit**.

Thus, the purified soul becomes the echo of divine will; a witness of the Vine's circulation expressed through word, sound, and vibration. Speech becomes **technology of the Spirit**; the living transmission of divine code.

Physiology — The Circulation of Fire

The human body became the new lampstand. Every believer was now a vessel of golden oil, the Spirit circulating within. Tongues of fire upon the head symbolised the **illumination of the mind**; the Spirit taking residence in human consciousness.

Just as blood carries life, **the Spirit carries truth**. The fire did not come to visit but to dwell, flowing from the inner man to the outer world like divine electricity through living wires. This is divine physiology: the nervous system of the Vine extended into the Body. Christ became the Head; the Church, His nerves and branches.

From that moment, every believer became a **bioluminescent vessel of Spirit**; God moving through human breath and body.

Chronology — The Day the Vine Multiplied

1. **At the Cross:** The Vine was wounded — blood and water flowed.

2. **At Resurrection:** The Vine revived — sap restored.

3. **At Pentecost:** The Vine multiplied — fire divided into branches.

4. **In the Church Age:** The Vine extends — Spirit flows to the nations.

5. **In the Sabbath Reign:** The Vine reigns — every branch bears fruit of glory.

Pentecost was the hinge between *individual redemption* and *corporate indwelling*. It was the moment when Christ's personal anointing became the Church's shared inheritance.

Technology — Communication as Living Extension of the Vine

This chapter carries the **technological revelation** of divine communication: Speech as *Spirit transmission*, not human articulation. Language, in God's system, is circuitry; the Vine's voice flowing through human frequency. Tongues were not random utterances but **living codes of communion**, bridging heaven and earth in real time.

The Spirit uses human sound as **biological technology**, turning lungs into wind instruments, tongues into conductors, and voices into rivers.

Thus, communication became **continuation**; the same Word that spoke creation now spoke through His Body. When the early believers spoke, creation recognised the sound; it was the same voice that said, *"Let there be light."*

Prophetic Application — Becoming the Outpouring

The outpouring did not end in *Acts 2*; it began. The Spirit never stops multiplying. Every believer is both a **recipient and extension** of Pentecost, a continuation of the fire.

To live as an outpouring branch means:

- To carry the same flame without containment.
- To speak as the Spirit breathes, not as the mind calculates.
- To become a living language of divine wisdom.
- To communicate heaven's mind to earth's confusion.
- To remain flammable — pure enough for the fire to dwell continually.

The true Pentecostal life is not shouting in power but **resting in fire**; a still flame, never quenched, never self-made.

Prophetic Declaration

"I am a living branch of the Vine of Fire.
The Word flows through my voice; the Spirit burns upon
my mind.
Every breath I take is communication between heaven
and earth.
I am not a vessel visited — I am a vessel inhabited.
The same fire that fell in Jerusalem burns within me.
I am the continuation of Pentecost, the
outpouring of the Vine into the nations."

CHAPTER 18

The Olive Branches of the Spirit:
The Witness (Romans 11)

Theme: Grafting into the Vine of Glory — The Reunion of Spirit and Nations in the Government of the Sabbath Age

The Mystery of Grafting — Spirit into Spirit

When Paul speaks of the wild olive branches being grafted into the good olive tree, he unveils not a cultural or ethnic merger but a spiritual engrafting; a reunification of the scattered breath of Adam back into the living Spirit of the Covenant. Israel, in this revelation, is not the human nation but the human spirit born of the Word — the root that received the covenant breath. The Gentiles, representing the dispersed souls of men, are not joined by bloodline but by Spirit-line.

> *"And if some of the branches be broken off, and*
> *thou, being a wild olive tree, wert grafted in*
> *among them... partakest of the root and fatness*
> *of the olive tree." — Romans 11:17 (KJV)*

To be grafted in is to be reconnected to the original current of divine life; the **Sabbath circulation** of the Spirit, where rest is government and holiness is inheritance.

Spiritology: The Root of Israel's Spirit

The **root** is Christ — the Word made Spirit — in whom the law, covenant, and life converge.
· The **root** contains divine law — the DNA of order and life.
· The **stem** channels that life through revelation and obedience.
· The **branches** manifest that life through fruit — righteousness and praise.

The true Israel, therefore, is the **Spirit-born rootline** that flows from the Word through the Spirit into the sons. The grafting of Gentiles symbolises the **return of nations to Spirit-origin;** the restoration of Adam's breath through the Vine of the Word.

The Sabbath age represents the maturity of this grafting; when every branch flows with the same Spirit of Rest, no longer striving in religion or flesh, but **governed by the indwelling Root of Peace.**

Soulogy: The Healing of Separation

The grafting process pierces the old bark — it cuts. That wound is the soul's repentance, where self-reliance breaks and surrender opens. Only then can the new life of the root flow through.

In this, grafting is both **surgery and sanctification**. The soul bleeds, but the Spirit breathes. Pride is peeled away so humility can receive the sap of grace.

Thus, the soul of man; long estranged from the Spirit through rebellion, becomes one with the divine circulation again.

"Boast not against the branches... thou bearest not

the root, but the root thee." — Romans 11:18

Every true grafted branch learns the humility of dependence, knowing that the **life is in the Root**, not in the leaf.

Theology: One Root, Many Branches — The Universal Sabbath Body

The olive tree reveals the **architecture of divine government**. There is one Root (the Spirit), one Vine (Christ), and many branches (sons of Zion). Together they form the **Body of the Vine**, which is the corporate Sabbath — the global sanctuary of divine order.

In this government:

- The **Spirit of the LORD** is the root of identity and dominion.

- The **Spirit of Wisdom and Understanding** flow as sap — revelation and comprehension.

- The **Spirit of Counsel and Might** form the structure — guidance and strength.

- The **Spirit of Knowledge and of the Fear of the LORD** mature the fruit — holiness and righteousness.

Through this sevenfold flow, the Vine of Glory governs all nations with **Sabbath justice and mercy**.

Chronology: From Abraham's Root to the Nations' Bloom

The promise to Abraham — "In thee shall all families of the earth be blessed" — reaches fulfilment in this grafting.
Each age represents a new phase of divine horticulture:

1. **Root planted** — in Abraham's faith.

2. **Stem revealed** — in Israel's covenant.

3. **Branch manifested** — in Christ.

4. **Sap outpoured** — in Pentecost.

5. **Branches multiplied** — in the nations.

6. **Fruit matured** — in the Sabbath reign.

The grafting completes the circle — from one man's faith to many nations' fullness, until the **whole earth becomes one vineyard of light**, rooted in the Spirit of Truth.

Typology: The Olive Tree and the Sabbath Kingdom

The olive tree is a symbol of **peace, anointing, and witness**.
Its oil fed the lamps of the Tabernacle; its branches crowned kings and sealed covenants.
Thus, in prophetic typology:

- The **Root** is the covenant Spirit.

- The **Oil** is the anointing of truth.

- The **Tree** is the Kingdom of God.

- The **Fruit** is the manifestation of righteousness in men.

When the grafting reaches its fullness, the tree becomes the **Tree of Life restored**, and the nations are healed by its leaves — the knowledge of the Holy.

"For if the casting away of them be the reconciling of the world, what shall the receiving of them be, but life from the dead?" — Romans 11:15

Prophetic Fulfilment: The Sabbath Vine of Glory

In the end, the olive branches are no longer divided.

The wild and the cultivated, the Gentile and the Hebrew, the soul and the spirit — all are united in one Vine. This is the **Body of the Branch**, the Sabbath Kingdom, where righteousness reigns, peace flows, and every nation drinks of the same oil of the Spirit.

This is the **Vine of Glory**, the living government of the Lamb and His Bride; rooted in Zion, branching through the earth, shining in eternal rest.

CHAPTER 19

*The Tree of Life Restored
(Revelation 22)*

Theme: The Full Circle of Life — From Branch to Tree, from Root to River

> *"In the midst of the street of it, and on either side
> of the river, was there the tree of life, which bare
> twelve manner of fruits, and yielded her fruit
> every month: and the leaves of the tree were for the
> healing of the nations." — Revelation 22:2 (KJV)*

Theology — The Fulfilled Covenant of Life

In Eden, the Tree of Life was barred; in Zion, it is reopened. Between Genesis and Revelation lies the history of pruning, grafting, and growing; until the Branch becomes the Tree that fills the nations. Here, the covenant of the Root of Jesse reaches full bloom: eternal communion between God and man. The throne of God and of the Lamb are no longer separated from the river; they are its source. Dominion is restored not by power, but by indwelling; the rule of righteousness flowing through rest. The Tree of Life is the Vine matured, the Branch glorified, the Word made body in every nation.

Spiritology — The River and the Flow of the Spirit

The river proceeding from the throne is not merely water; it is *Spirit in motion*, the eternal Sabbath current. What was once oil in the candlestick and blood in the covenant becomes now living water; the Spirit's final manifestation as flow. Each branch that once abided in the Vine becomes a tributary of this river, carrying healing to the nations. The Spirit's government is no longer confined to temple or tribe; it flows through the redeemed body of the Bride, the habitation of God.

The Sabbath finds its perfection not in stillness alone, but in the *restful flow* of divine life; motion without labour, fruitfulness without toil.

Soulogy — The Twelve Fruits of Rulership

Twelve fruits; one for each month, one for each tribe, one for each dimension of divine order. This is the soul perfected: every season producing its ordained fruit, no longer withering under time. Where once the soul fluctuated between faith and fear, now it abides in rhythm with eternity. Each fruit is a revelation, each month a new expression of the everlasting Word. The healed soul no longer resists pruning; it has become a tree itself, yielding willingly to the sap of the Spirit.

The healed soul becomes the leaf of healing; its submission to the Spirit releases medicine to nations.

Physiology — The Body as the Tree of Healing

The "leaves of the tree" are not mere symbols; they represent the living bodies of the redeemed, transfigured as vessels of divine light and fragrance. The glorified body becomes a branch of healing; every cell, every breath, releases restoration.

The redeemed no longer need the sun, for the *Spirit of*

Light illuminates them from within. The body itself becomes a riverbed, carrying divine vitality through eternity.

As the body once bore the image of the earthly, it now bears the image of the heavenly — a physiology of glory.

Typology — The Circle Completed

The Branch from the root of Jesse (*Isaiah 11:1*) has become the Tree of Life (*Revelation 22*). The candlestick of Exodus has become the river of light. The rod that budded has become the garden restored. The covenant that once required priests now lives in kings.

This is the divine cycle fulfilled: **Root → Branch → Vine → Tree → River → Throne**.
The order of creation restored through the order of resurrection.

Chronology — The Eternal Sabbath

The story began on the sixth day with man made in God's image. It ends in the seventh — the eternal Sabbath — where man rests in God's likeness. No evening, no morning. Just *abiding*. The Kingdom's reign is perpetual peace, the government of the Spirit manifest in eternal rhythm.

The Sabbath is no longer a day, but a dwelling; no longer a law, but a life.

Prophetic View — The Sons of the Tree

The sons of Zion now stand as branches of this Tree of Life. The same Spirit that once anointed prophets now flows as inheritance. Their words are fruit; their intercession, leaves; their life, the riverbed of divine healing. The nations no longer resist the Branch; they drink from it. And the Lamb, the Root and the Offspring, reigns through them forever.

Application — Living as the Tree

To live as the Tree of Life is to let the river of the Spirit flow through every part of your being: thought, word, and action. It is to be so joined with the Vine that your fruit becomes healing for others, your presence a fountain of peace.
The Branch of Righteousness has now become the Body of Rest — **the Tree of Life restored in man**.

"Blessed are they that do His commandments, that they may have right to the tree of life." (Revelation 22:14)

CHAPTER 20

The Vine of the Lamb

Theme: The Eternal Circulation of Life — The Spirit and the Bride as One Flow

> *"I am the Vine, ye are the branches: he that abideth in Me, and I in him, the same bringeth forth much fruit: for without Me ye can do nothing." — John 15:5 (KJV)*
> *"For the Lamb which is in the midst of the throne shall feed them, and shall lead them unto living fountains of waters." — Revelation 7:17 (KJV)*

The Vine of the Lamb — Life Enthroned

The final revelation of Christ is not the suffering Servant nor only the reigning King, but the living Vine enthroned as the Lamb. This is the mystery of gentle dominion; power through yielding, victory through indwelling. The Lamb rules not by decree but by life; He governs through circulation. His kingdom is a living organism: Spirit flowing through body, Word through vessel, love through all. The Vine of the Lamb is the government of life; not imposed from above, but breathed from within. The throne itself becomes a heart; its rule, a pulse.

The blood that once redeemed now circulates eternally as Spirit-life.

Spiritology — Circulation of Divine Life through Spirit and Word

The Spirit is the blood of the Vine; the Word is its sap. Together they create divine circulation; an eternal flow of communion between Creator and creation. What began in the Garden as breath returns in Revelation as a river. The Spirit moves through the branches as living energy, keeping every soul joined to the Vine's pulse.

This is the *Law of Eternal Flow*:

- The Spirit flows from the Father through the Son.

- The Word abides in the Vine.

- The branches receive and bear the same current of life.

No separation, no stagnation — only perpetual exchange. As blood carries oxygen to every cell, so the Spirit carries revelation to every part of the Body. Every truth spoken from the Vine revives the branch; every prayer returned from the branch refreshes the Vine.

The Church is not an institution; it is the living bloodstream of Christ.

Soulogy — Zion and Jerusalem within

In the Vine of the Lamb, the geography of the soul is healed. The divided self; mind against heart becomes a unified garden of rest.

- **Zion** represents the renewed mind: the hill of divine thought, elevated above confusion, where wisdom reigns.

- **Jerusalem** represents the purified heart: the dwelling of peace, where love is enthroned.

When the mind (Zion) and the heart (Jerusalem) are reconciled, man becomes the habitation of the Vine; Spirit and truth intertwined.

The Vine grows where thought and affection no longer war, but worship together.

In this inner city, Christ reigns as both light and warmth; wisdom guiding, love sustaining. The soul becomes luminous, not merely informed.

Theology — The Lamb as Root, Vine, and Fruit

Christ is the Alpha and the Omega of life's continuum:

- As **Root**, He anchors creation in eternity.

- As **Vine**, He channels Spirit through communion.

- As **Fruit**, He reveals the sweetness of obedience.

The Lamb's government is organic; every command flows as nourishment, not burden. Law becomes life; obedience becomes growth. The Vine teaches without coercion, shapes without domination.

The Lamb's authority is the mastery of gentleness; the power to make all life fruitful through love.

This is the restoration of divine ecology: no waste, no striving, only circulation. Every branch finds its measure, every fruit its season, every drop its source in Him.

Typology — From Blood to Spirit, From Cup to River

At the Supper, Christ gave the cup and said, *"This is my blood."* In the Vine, that cup becomes a river; the same essence now multiplied across eternity. The wine of communion becomes the life of the Lamb, ever flowing through the redeemed.

Each believer becomes a chalice of His flow, a vessel of circulation. To drink of the Vine is not to receive once, but to remain in the stream. Every act of worship, every word of truth, keeps the current alive.

The Vine's wine is not symbolic; it is Spirit made tangible in fellowship.

Prophetic End — The Branch Now Reigns through the Vine

The Vine of the Lamb is the final revelation of union; *the Spirit and the Bride saying, Come.* What was once separation between Creator and creation dissolves into communion. The Branch (Christ) that once grew from Jesse's root now extends through every redeemed soul; the Vine multiplied, the Body glorified.

The reign of the Lamb is not a government of laws but of life. He reigns through fruit, not force; through Spirit, not sword. Every branch that abides becomes an instrument of His reign; not merely worshipping Him, but expressing Him. The Branch now reigns through the Vine; man and God breathing as one life.

This is the eternal Sabbath: the circulation of peace that never ends, the Kingdom where the Word and Spirit are one, where every heart beats in rhythm with the Lamb's pulse.

Application — Living in the Circulation of the Lamb

To live as part of the Vine of the Lamb is to live as an open vessel; no dams, no resistance. When the Spirit speaks, flow. When the Word convicts, yield. When the Vine prunes, trust. This is not religion but respiration; the rhythm of divine exchange.

Abiding is not effort; it is surrender to flow. The branch never strains to bear fruit; it simply stays connected to the pulse of the Vine.

The goal of redemption was never merely forgiveness; it was circulation.

That through the Lamb, divine life might finally move freely again.

BONUS PART

THE CROWNED VINE: THE FINAL REVELATION OF THE BRANCH

Theme: The Fire Becomes Fruit, the Branch Becomes the Vine

BONUS CHAPTER 1

The Branch Restored in
Glory (Zechariah 3–6)

Theme: Priest and King United in One Root

Priesthood and Kingship fused in the fire of intercession and crowned in the glory of dominion.

1. Spirit of the LORD — The Anointing of the Dual Crown

Dimension: Spiritology

The Spirit of the LORD descends as **the governing presence**, joining priesthood and kingship into one flow. This Spirit lifts Joshua from accusation and empowers Zerubbabel for completion. The same anointing that sanctifies the altar strengthens the hands that build the temple.

> *"The counsel of peace shall be between*
> *them both." (Zechariah 6:13)*

The Branch does not choose between priestly mercy or kingly rule; it embodies both. The Spirit of the LORD is the **seal of unity;** the power of divine equilibrium. Through this Spirit, the

Branch becomes a **living conduit of God's presence**, the dwelling of rest and rule combined.

Prophetic Essence:
Where the Spirit of the LORD rests, dominion flows without striving; authority becomes intercession, and glory is expressed as rest.

2. Spirit of Wisdom — The Fusion of Function and Fire

Dimension: Theology

The Spirit of Wisdom instructs how to wear the crown and wield the sceptre without corruption. Joshua's mitre signifies sanctified intellect; the mind ruled by divine counsel. Zerubbabel's plumbline symbolises discernment; the measure of divine alignment.

> *"Who art thou, O great mountain? Before Zerubbabel thou shalt become a plain." (Zechariah 4:7)*

Wisdom turns obstacles into altars; resistance into revelation. It reveals that rulership is not achieved by conquest, but by conformity to divine design. The Branch becomes wise not by study but by **abiding in divine structure**.

Prophetic Essence:
Wisdom is the architecture of divine governance; the ability to build with eternity in view.

3. Spirit of Understanding — The Light Between the Olive Trees

Dimension: Soulogy

In Zechariah's vision, two olive trees pour oil into the golden bowl that feeds the seven lamps. These are the two anointed ones "the priestly and the kingly flows" united in continual supply. Understanding is the recognition of how Spirit circulates through function.

> *"These are the two anointed ones, that stand by*
> *the Lord of the whole earth." (Zechariah 4:14)*

Understanding unites heart and mind; Jerusalem and Zion; feeling and revelation. It is the soul's awakening to divine circulation; the **flow of oil through consciousness**.

Prophetic Essence:
When the soul understands its position in the Vine, the flow never ceases; prayer becomes breathing, and revelation becomes rest.

4. Spirit of Counsel — The Crown of Intercession

Dimension: Typology

The crown placed upon Joshua's head was not ornamental; it was **functional counsel**. It signified the weight of spiritual responsibility carried in prayer.

Counsel transforms authority into ministry. The Branch does not command by decree alone; it **rules by communion**. The Spirit of Counsel makes governance a dialogue; heaven and earth conversing through a yielded vessel.

> *"And the counsel of peace shall be between*
> *them both." (Zechariah 6:13)*

Prophetic Essence:
Counsel is the government of compassion; it rules through listening and guides through mercy.

5. Spirit of Might — The Hands that Finish

Dimension: Physiology

> *"The hands of Zerubbabel have laid the*
> *foundation of this house; his hands shall*
> *also finish it." (Zechariah 4:9)*

The Spirit of Might establishes the physical execution of divine will. Here, the human vessel becomes the **ground of glory**, where divine energy finds embodiment. What began in prayer manifests in performance.

Physiologically, Might represents the sanctification of action; the muscles of obedience, the endurance of faith. The Branch's strength is not human stamina but divine infusion: **Spirit animating flesh** without corruption.

Prophetic Essence:
True might is the ability to finish without fatigue; divine perseverance in human form.

6. Spirit of Knowledge — The Revelation of the Hidden Stone

Dimension: Chronology

> *"Upon one stone shall be seven eyes... and I will*
> *engrave the graving thereof." (Zechariah 3:9)*

Knowledge here is not merely information, but rather **illumination of divine timing**. The stone with seven eyes represents the omniscient oversight of God: His plan engraved in history, His pattern observed by the seven Spirits.
Chronologically, the Branch appears in the fullness of time,

when the priesthood has been purified and the kingship prepared.

Prophetic Essence:
Knowledge is the unveiling of divine seasons; the awareness that every fire has purpose and every waiting carries weight.

7. Spirit of the Fear of the LORD — The Reverence of Rest

Dimension: Application

The culmination of the Branch's restoration is reverence; the awe that sustains balance. To bear the crown and wield the sceptre is a fearful honour. The fear of the LORD guards glory from pride.

This Spirit maintains the Branch's posture of worship even while reigning. It remembers that fire was first judgment before it became favour; that rule must remain rooted in righteousness.

> *"In that day, saith the LORD of hosts, shall ye call every man his neighbour under the vine and under the fig tree." (Zechariah 3:10)*

Fear of the LORD keeps the Branch fruitful — humble, luminous, and continually dependent.

Prophetic Essence:
Reverence is the root of rest; the crown that bows becomes the crown that reigns.

Final Revelation: The Crowned Branch Becomes the Lamp of the Temple

Through the operation of the seven Spirits, the Branch becomes the **living menorah** of divine government. Priesthood and kingship are not parallel offices but **interwoven currents** of one light. The fire that once consumed now illuminates; the throne that once judged now intercedes.

The Branch restored in glory stands as **the prophetic blueprint of Christ in His Body;** a company of sons who reign through prayer, build through purity, and shine through humility.

> *"He shall bear the glory, and shall sit and rule upon his throne; and the counsel of peace shall be between them both." (Zechariah 6:13)*

BONUS CHAPTER 2

The Branch in the Fire
(Ezekiel 15; Malachi 4:1)

Theme: Purging before Bloom — fire as the horticulture of heaven

the vine fit only for fuel (Ezekiel 15) and ...
the day that burns like an oven, and the Sun of
righteousness arising with healing (Malachi 4:1–2)

Opening: Fire Is God's Horticulture

The scripture that scares the proud is the word that trains the humble. Ezekiel shows the vine that is useless for building: wood that becomes fuel. Malachi speaks of a day that burns like an oven; a time when the mixture is exposed and only sanctified gold remains. These images are terrifying to those who love veneer; they are liberating to those who love root. Fire is not arbitrary annihilation. It is the heavenly method of extracting life from dead form, of separating seed from chaff so the true stock may multiply.

1. Typology — The Vine without Fruit Becomes the Kindling of

Renewal

The vine has two destinies in prophetic economy: to bear fruit or to feed the flame. When the branch refuses the Vine's sap, when faith dries into form and leaves hide instead of feed — it ceases to be instrument and becomes kindling.

- The fruitless vine is judgment's fuel.

- The fruitful vine is the temple's lamp.

This is not cruelty. It is a classification. The burning of dead wood creates heat for the pot that cooks the new bread. God repurposes waste into means for refining. The church that fears fire mistakes culling for cruelty; the remnant knows that kindling pays for the bread of the next season.

2. Spiritology — Judgment as Mercy: The Fire Consumes Decay but Preserves Seed

Spiritually, fire is the refining hand of God. Malachi's oven and Ezekiel's flame function as mercy in action.

- **Consuming Flame:** it removes what cannot carry life; hypocrisy, religious performance, self-trust.

- **Refining Flame:** it burns away the mixture so the gold, the life-bearing core, remains.

- **Preserving Flame:** paradoxically, the seed that carries covenant life is sheltered and emerges more potent from the heat.

The Holy Spirit does not waste suffering. He uses it to refine identity: what seemed loss is often the concentration of destiny. Judgment, here, is the surgical strike that spares the remnant and prepares labourers for harvest.

3. Soulogy — Burning as Transformation of Desire

At the level of the soul, fire recalibrates desire. Many people confess fear, but what they truly fear is loss of image. The inward flame strips the soul of idols; the craving for approval, gain, control.

- **Desire re-ordered:** the appetite for glory is replaced by hunger for God.

- **Love purified:** attachments that masqueraded as devotion burn away until love becomes simple and fierce.

- **Will surrendered:** the will learns to permit pruning rather than perform preservation.

This burning is not masochistic. It is formative. The soul that allows the furnace becomes pliable; the selfish walls drop; the secret rooms of the heart open and begin to receive true light.

4. Physiology — The Body as Altar, the Flesh as Fuel or Vessel

Ezekiel's vine image charges the body with two possibilities: to be used (temple) or to be consumed (fuel). The fire touches flesh and physiology.

- **Fuelled Flesh:** the unrepentant body feeds the old patterns; lust, appetite, control, and thus becomes fuel.

- **Vessel Flesh:** a yielded body becomes altar; blood, breath, nerve-conducting Spirit instead of resisting it.

Healing can feel like heat: detox, withdrawal, relational breakdowns. But physiologically, these are often the Spirit reorganising neural pathways; rewiring appetite to receive Spirit rather than satisfy the old self. The brave let the body be reconfigured; the fearful resurrect the old branches.

5. Theology — Fire's Place in Covenant Reality

Theologically, God's covenant includes purging. Covenant is not a sentimental promise to exempt us from correction; it is a guarantee that discipline will produce children.

- God's justice is redemptive.

- His refining is covenantal: *He does not burn what He will not restore.*

- The Day of the Lord (Malachi's oven) distinguishes retribution from remediation: the proud are consumed; the humble are healed by the Sun of righteousness.

Therefore, the furnace is not proof of abandonment but proof of ownership. The God who disciplines does so to perfect sons who can govern without idolatry.

6. Chronology — The Pattern Through History: Pruning, Fall, Fire, and Flower

History cycles through pruning and flowering:

- Fall and corruption produce dead wood (Ezekiel's vine).

- Nations and systems that refuse repentance fuel judgment (Malachi's day).

- From the ashes, God preserves a root (the remnant).

- The preserved root re-springs into a purified branch that bears brighter fruit.

This chronological law repeats from Eden to Eden restored: the pattern is pruning → pressure → purification → proliferation.

7. Typology — Biblical Pictures: From the Fig Tree to the Furnace

Scriptural types echo the same truth:

- The fig tree that withered under judgment (**Mark 11**) =

religious form without life.

- The bush that burned but did not consume (Exodus) = a holy paradox of presence through purification.

- The refiner's fire (Malachi) = covenantal purification that ends with healing.

These types teach the believer how to interpret inner and outer fires: not as punishments alone but as prophetic instruments of reform.

8. Technology — How the Spirit Uses Fire Practically

If fire is God's method, what is His "technology" for implementing it in human lives and communities?

- **Language of Loss:** God often allows the removal of idols through loss—job, reputation, relationship—so hearts unclench.

- **Structural Collapse:** institutions that ossify are allowed to fail so new forms can be built (Zerubbabel's rebuilding after ruin).

- **Purifying Disciplines:** fasting, solitude, and prophetic truth function as conduits for the refining flame.

- **Communal Pressures:** corporate testing—persecution, exile —functions like a furnace that cleanses a people.

These aren't abstract. They are the operating system God uses to take what is soft and noble and make it unassailable.

9. Application — How to Stand in the Fire Without Becoming Fuel

This is the practical, pastoral core. Most people either run from fire or lean into masochism. The wise posture is: *remain but yield.*

Practical steps:

1. **Name the Heat:** acknowledge what you are feeling—loss, shame, rage—without hiding it.

2. **Refuse Self-Justification:** repentance opens doors; justification hardens wood.

3. **Offer the Heart as a Vessel:** consciously surrender areas of control to God — let the Spirit rewire desire.

4. **Keep Communion:** maintain the discipline of Word, worship, and small obedience — these carry oil into the flame and prevent destruction.

5. **Expect Refining, Not Rejection:** interpret the pain as belonging, not abandonment.

6. **Watch for Seed-Preservation:** look for the small unburnt kernel—promise, call, talent—that persists. That is your covenant seed.

7. **Seek Community that Prays:** fire is safe under faithful hands; the Body intercedes and receives revelation in fire.

Remember: *only dry branches fear it.* The living branch learns to offer itself and trusts that God will return what He refines multiplied.

10. Prophetic Conclusion — From Burning to Beauty

The chapter closes with the promise: fire that burns without devouring is God's merciful act. Malachi's darker word ends with the Sun of righteousness rising with healing in his wings. The furnace is not the end; it is the crucible of the Bride.

The Branch that endures the fire becomes light-bearing. The wood that would have been kindling is transmuted into the framework of the temple. Judgment, when worn rightly, becomes the wardrobe of glory.

11. Declaration

> *"Refiner, perfect the Branch in me. Burn my dead leaves; keep my root. Let whatever is fuel go to the flame, but preserve, purify, and multiply the seed that bears Your name. In the oven of Your purpose, make me bread for the nations."*

BONUS CHAPTER 3

The Rod and the Root:
From Branch to Vine

Theme: *Maturity of the Pattern — Incarnation of Life*

"A rod shall come forth out of the stem of Jesse, and a Branch shall grow out of his roots." — Isaiah 11:1

Opening: The Rod Becomes the Vine

Every divine pattern begins as a seed, matures into a branch, and culminates in a vine; a living continuum where root and fruit are no longer separate. In the prophetic ages, the rod in Moses' hand was authority delegated; in Christ, the Vine became authority embodied.

The Word that once spoke from heaven now flows through flesh. What was symbol has become substance; what was touch has become habitation. The journey from rod to vine is the journey of **incarnation;** from *representation* to *union*, from *authority wielded* to *life shared.*

1. Chronology — From the Rod of Moses to the Vine of Christ

God's dealings with man trace a living timeline of maturation:

- **The Rod of Moses (*Exodus 4–14*):**
The rod was an external symbol of delegated power. It struck waters, parted seas, and judged Egypt — a picture of divine authority moving *through* a chosen vessel, but not *abiding in* him.

- **The Rod of Aaron (*Numbers 17*):**
Here, the rod buds, blossoms, and bears almonds — a sign that authority is no longer just positional but *life-giving*. Resurrection life begins to appear. The dead staff becomes a living branch.

- **The Root of Jesse (*Isaiah 11*):**
The covenant narrows into one lineage — a root preserved through decay. What began as a wooden rod (law and command) now carries sap (Spirit and promise).

- **The Vine of Christ (*John 15*):**
Finally, authority and life are united. The Vine does not need to strike or bloom externally; it *circulates life internally*. This is the transition from *commandment* to *communion*.

Thus, the chronology unfolds:
Rod — Branch — Root — Vine — Tree of Life.
Each phase brings the pattern closer to embodiment, until God no longer stands apart from His people but *flows within them*.

2. Theology — The Word Made Flesh: Divine Sap in Human Vessel

Theologically, this chapter marks the mystery of the Incarnation. The **Rod of Word** became the **Vine of Spirit**. The eternal Word took on matter and breathed Spirit into mortality.

- The **rod** was authority **declared**.

- The **Vine** is authority **shared**.

Christ did not just demonstrate power; He distributed it through connection. His flesh became the conduit through which divine nature entered the human bloodstream. The sap of heaven began to pulse through veins of dust.

In Him, the invisible Root and visible Branch meet; heaven and earth reconciled in one organism.
Thus, the Vine is the **fusion of divine essence and human obedience**, the living proof that Spirit can fully inhabit form without corruption.

3. Spiritology — Indwelling, Not Visiting

The Spirit's movement also matures in this transition. In the era of the Rod, the Spirit came **upon** men. In the era of the Vine, He lives **within** them.

- The rod carried *visitation*.

- The vine carries *habitation*.

In Moses, the rod's power was borrowed. In Christ, the Vine's power is intrinsic; the Spirit flows as His nature. Thus, Pentecost becomes the distribution of that inner sap: *tongues of fire* upon heads marking the same current that flowed in the Vine now flowing in every branch.

The branch does not visit the Vine for strength; it lives by continual union. This is the end of external religion and the birth of spiritual life.

The Spirit no longer visits; He circulates. He no longer anoints for a moment; He abides forever.

4. Typology — The Tree of Life Reappears in Emmanuel

Typologically, Christ fulfils and restores Eden's central mystery. The Tree of Life, once guarded by cherubim, now reappears in **Emmanuel — God with us.**

- In Eden, man reached *toward* the Tree.

- In Christ, the Tree reaches *into* man.

The cross itself becomes the intersection of root and branch; the Rod lifted up becomes the Vine stretched out. The crucifixion is the grafting of humanity into divinity: wood pierced by Spirit, blood mingled with life.

Christ is both **Root and Fruit**, **Rod and Vine**, **Seed and Tree**. In Him, all parts of the pattern reconcile: the authority of heaven (rod) flows through the nourishment of grace (vine), producing eternal fruit: the sons of God.

5. Soulogy — Yielding Individuality to Become One Life

At the soul level, this transition is the death of independence and the birth of participation. Every branch must one day **yield its individuality**; not to lose identity, but to be perfected in unity.

When self-will dies, divine will circulates unhindered. When personal ambition ceases, divine sap begins to flow. The mature soul no longer asks, "How can I serve?" but rather, "How can I remain?"

To abide is higher than to achieve.
To flow is greater than to strive.

The vine-life replaces performance with communion, effort with essence, striving with resting. The soul becomes a conduit of divine circulation; thinking, feeling, and desiring as extensions of God's heart.

6. Physiology — The Body as Living Vine

Physiologically, the incarnation sanctifies the body as the living rootbed of God's Spirit.
In the Vine, the human body becomes an organ of divine flow.

- The **bloodstream** carries the sap of the Spirit — life circulating from heart to heart.

- The **breath** becomes divine respiration — God exhaling through man.

- The **hands** become branches of touch — extending the tenderness of Christ.

The Vine sanctifies flesh; not to glorify carnality, but to redeem it as a vessel of divine life. Thus, the Church as the Body is not metaphor only; it is the physiology of the Vine on earth.

7. Prophetic Vision — From Rod to Vine to Crown

Prophetically, this movement completes the restoration cycle:

- The **Rod** represents the Word's command.

- The **Branch** represents the Word's growth.

- The **Vine** represents the Word's communion.

- The **Crown** represents the Word's dominion.

By the time the Vine blossoms fully in the sons of Zion, the Rod of iron (**Psalm 2:9**) has become the Vine of life (**Revelation 22:2**). What began as discipline now becomes delight. The law of command becomes the law of communion; written not on tablets, but in hearts.

8. Application — Becoming One Vine with Him

To walk in this mystery is to live beyond separation. The mature believer understands that:

- You are not a servant holding His rod, but a branch sharing His life.

- You do not *carry* the Spirit; the Spirit *circulates* through you.

- The Word is not *studied* for strength; it *flows* as sap in meditation, prayer, and obedience.

Practical posture for this maturity:

1. **Abide continually.** Remain in stillness; divine flow thrives in rest.

2. **Yield completely.** Let no area remain unrooted in His will.

3. **Flow freely.** Don't hoard revelation; circulation keeps life alive.

4. **Bear fruit quietly.** Vine-life is not noisy; its power is consistency.

Every mature branch reaches this point: **to become indistinguishable from the Vine.** That is not loss; that is perfection.

9. Prophetic Conclusion — The Vine of God's Dwelling

The rod once ruled Egypt; the Vine now rules creation. The same authority that struck the Nile now nourishes nations. The same Word that judged Pharaoh now heals the world.

The Rod commanded.
The Branch obeyed.
The Vine abides.

In Christ, the pattern is complete: the government of Spirit no longer descends by decree but flows by indwelling. The Tree of Life has grown again, not in Eden's soil but in the heart of every redeemed son.

Declaration

"O Vine of eternal life, let me cease from striving and

begin to flow.
Make me one root with You, one sap, one sound, one
song.
Let every rod of command within me bend into the Vine
of communion.
In Your life I live; in Your flow I flourish;
in Your union I reign."

BONUS CHAPTER 4

*The Voice in the Vine: Job's
Cry in the Furnace*

Theme: Revelation Born of Suffering

The Hidden Word in the Furnace

Before there was Scripture written, there was Scripture spoken through fire. Job stands as the earliest human scroll of endurance; a living prophecy of how the Vine speaks through the flame. His cry is not rebellion; it is revelation struggling for language in the pressure of purification. In him, we see the Voice of the Vine—Christ's eternal Word—forming its first articulation through human suffering. The furnace is not a punishment; it is a *microcosm of the Cross*, where the Word within man meets the weight of divine silence, and out of that silence, the voice of revelation is born.

Soulogy: The Language of Pain Becomes Prophecy

When Job cried, "Though He slay me, yet will I trust in Him" (*Job 13:15*), his soul was not lamenting; it was translating. Pain became the alphabet of prophecy. The soul, once divided between faith and despair, learns through trial to synchronise with Spirit's rhythm. The tears become syllables of truth, and grief becomes grammar for glory.

In suffering, the human soul is stretched until it touches its eternal dimension. This is why Job's pain speaks beyond his century; it was never personal agony alone, but *universal articulation*. The soul's suffering becomes a mirror of the Spirit's groaning within creation (**Romans 8:22–23**).

Every furnace rewrites the language of the soul. When purified, emotion becomes discernment, and lament becomes liturgy.

Spiritology: The Vine Speaks Through Endurance

The Vine's power is not seen in ease but in endurance. The sap of divine life flows strongest when pressure mounts against it. When Job sat in ashes, scraping himself with broken pottery, heaven was not silent; it was listening. The Spirit's flow within him was turning pain into prophecy.

The Vine endures every pruning and every flame without losing its root. Thus, endurance is not passive survival; it is the *flow of Spirit* refusing interruption.
When the Spirit abides, every wound becomes a well, every tear becomes oil, and every silence becomes speech.

Suffering, for those grafted into the Vine, is not a disconnection but a deeper sap exchange; the Spirit transmitting divine virtue through the vessel's cracks.

Theology: Suffering Does Not Silence the Word — It Purifies Its Tone

Job's story teaches that divine revelation passes through *refinement before release.* God's Word cannot dwell fully in untested vessels. Fire is the *theological necessity* for pure speech. When God allowed Job to be tried, He was not proving Job's weakness but preparing His own voice in man.

Christ fulfilled this mystery on the Cross when He cried, "My God, My God, why hast Thou forsaken Me?" (*Matthew 27:46*). This was not loss of faith; it was the *Voice of the Vine* echoing Job's cry, proving that divine union does not exempt us from suffering; it transforms suffering into intercession.

Every true revelation must first be baptized in pain. Truth that has not passed through fire remains academic; only truth tempered by trial carries *the tone of eternity*.

Typology: Job's Cry Anticipates Christ's Groan on the Cross

Job and Jesus mirror one mystery: the Word refining the vessel through the furnace.

- **Job's ashes** prefigure **Gethsemane's agony**.

- **His boils** prefigure **Christ's stripes**.

- **His friends' accusations** prefigure **the Pharisees' mockery**.

- **His restoration** prefigures **Christ's resurrection**.

Both are branches tested by fire to reveal the life of the Vine. When Job said, "I know that my Redeemer liveth" (*Job 19:25*), he was seeing Christ before the Incarnation; the Root rising from his ashes. In both cases, the furnace becomes the womb of revelation.

Application: The Furnace Is the Classroom of Articulation

Do not flee the furnace; it is the voice-chamber of God. Every disciple who would *speak light* must first *bleed truth*. The trial you endure is not your destruction but your translation—God rewriting your sound to match His tone.

If you yield in the fire:

- Your *mind* will burn with understanding.

- Your *heart* will glow with compassion.

- Your *speech* will resonate with heaven's frequency.

The furnace is where the *Word in you* becomes the *Word through you.* It is where silence births sound, where tears anoint truth, and where the Vine learns to sing through your voice.

Prophetic End: The Vine Speaks as Man

When Job's trial ended, he saw God: not in thunder, but in the quiet whisper that remained after the storm. The Voice in the Vine had completed its circuit, from Root (God) to Branch (man) and back again. This is the destiny of all who abide in the Vine: to become the living voice of divine endurance, speaking life even from the ashes.

> *"When He hath tried me, I shall come*
> *forth as gold." —Job 23:10*

Gold speaks without words. It is silent fire; purity that remembers pain but no longer feels it. Such is the *voice of the Vine*: revelation born of suffering, crowned in light, speaking forever from within the eternal Root.

BONUS CHAPTER 5

*The Vine of Understanding: Wisdom
as the Inner Wine (Proverbs 3–9)*

Theme: Intimacy with Wisdom — Drinking from the Inner Cup

The Secret Wine of Light

The Book of Proverbs unveils a secret vineyard hidden in the soul; the Vine of Understanding, where divine light ferments into comprehension. Wisdom is not an external tutor but an internal vintner; she crushes the grapes of revelation until the soul begins to drink illumination, not as thought, but as experience.

> *"Wisdom hath builded her house, she hath*
> *hewn out her seven pillars... she hath*
> *mingled her wine" (Proverbs 9:1–2).*

This mingled wine is not worldly intellect but the *distilled essence of divine light;* the fermented Word matured through intimacy with the Spirit.

Wisdom is the Spirit's voice when love becomes understanding, and understanding becomes rest. It is the *wine of comprehension* that intoxicates the mind of Christ within man, teaching him to see as God sees, to feel as God feels, and to discern as God discerns.

Spiritology: Wisdom as the Distilled Light of Divine Life — The Wine of Comprehension

In spiritology, wisdom is the movement of divine light through consciousness. It is not a product of thought but a *vibration of union* between the Spirit of truth and the spirit of man. As wine is the concentration of a grape's essence, wisdom is the *distillation of God's life;* the Word that has ripened under the heat of revelation and matured into understanding.

When the Spirit of Wisdom descends, she does not bring new information; she *translates revelation into realisation.* She turns hearing into knowing and knowing into being. This is why Proverbs calls her a woman; not because of gender, but because she *conceives light* and *births insight.* She embodies the nurturing nature of the Spirit, the motherly essence of divine counsel.

The Vine of Understanding, therefore, is the continual flow of wisdom-wine from God's mind into the believer's spirit. When we abide in the Vine, we are invited to *drink the mind of Christ (**1 Corinthians 2:16**).*

Soulogy: The Heart Learns to Taste Truth, Not Merely to Know It

The soul's role in wisdom is not analytical but *sensory.* It learns to *taste truth.* **Psalm 34:8** says, "O taste and see that the Lord is good." To taste is to discern flavour; to perceive essence beyond form.

When the heart matures, it moves from *knowledge of God* to the *savour of God.* Wisdom teaches the heart to enjoy what truth feels like; to sense the sweetness of obedience, the aroma of righteousness, the warmth of mercy.

In this intimacy, the soul becomes like a tongue trained by the Spirit. Every word, every encounter, every revelation becomes a sip of divine wine. Soulish desire, once corrupted by lust for pleasure, is re-educated by Wisdom to desire *divine delight*.

Thus, the heart becomes a chalice, and love becomes the wine poured within it.

Physiology: Understanding Becomes Nourishment — Mind and Nerve Quickened by Revelation

Understanding is not just intellectual; it is *physiological in manifestation*. When divine wisdom enters the human system, it alters the body's rhythm. The mind quickens, perception sharpens, and peace becomes the body's new pulse.

Proverbs 3:8 declares, "It shall be health to thy navel, and marrow to thy bones." The Word received in wisdom does not rest in the mind; it circulates like blood. It strengthens the nervous system with divine order, aligning the physical vessel with spiritual vibration.

The human body, as the temple of the Spirit, becomes the vineyard where wisdom's wine ferments. Revelation, when obeyed, releases energy; a spiritual metabolism that renews strength and restores clarity.

Thus, wisdom is not only light to the spirit and sweetness to the soul but also *life to the flesh*. The more one abides in understanding, the more divine circulation flows freely through every fibre of being.

Typology: The Woman Wisdom Foreshadows the Bride Who Drinks from the Same Cup

Wisdom, personified as a woman in Proverbs, foreshadows the end-time Bride of Christ; the *Church of Understanding*. Both invite to the same table: "Come, eat of my bread, and drink of the wine which I have mingled" (**Proverbs 9:5**). This table is the altar of communion where revelation becomes relationship.

As Wisdom calls from the high places, so does the Spirit and the Bride say, "Come" (**Revelation 22:17**).
In this prophetic typology, *Wisdom is the Spirit preparing the Bride to drink from the inner cup.*

The seven pillars of her house (**Proverbs 9:1**) correspond to the seven Spirits of God in **Isaiah 11:2**; one of which is the Spirit of Wisdom and Understanding. The Bride, crowned with these seven, becomes the completed vessel of divine light — the woman who has drunk deeply of the inner wine and now speaks with the voice of the Vine.

Application: True Wisdom Is Not Information but Fermentation — Word Aged into Spirit

Knowledge is grape; wisdom is wine. Between the two lie time, pressure, and stillness. Wisdom is the *Word aged into Spirit;* revelation that has fermented in obedience, silence, and experience.

Do not rush divine understanding. Let revelation sit in your heart until it matures into light. Meditation is fermentation; when stillness allows the Spirit to transform what you know into what you *are.*

When the Vine of Understanding fills you:

• You stop reacting and begin discerning.

• You stop striving and begin abiding.

• You stop memorising truth and begin becoming truth.

To drink from this cup is to let the Word dwell richly (*Colossians 3:16*) until your perception changes flavour. You will know when it happens, peace becomes your aftertaste.

Prophetic End: The Inner Wine of Rest

The Vine of Understanding leads to the Sabbath of Wisdom, a rest where the mind ceases striving and simply *knows as it is known.* The believer who drinks this wine begins to see the world not as a battlefield of confusion but as a vineyard of divine order.

In this rest:

- Thought becomes prayer.

- Perception becomes communion.

- Every action flows from revelation, not reaction.

This is the maturity of the Branch; when wisdom and love blend into one wine, and the soul drinks deeply of divine comprehension.

"Wisdom hath mingled her wine." — Proverbs 9:2

This is the cup of the Spirit; the inner wine of understanding, shared only with those who dwell long enough in silence to taste eternity.

BONUS CHAPTER 6

*The Vine and the
Husbandman (John 15)*

Theme: The Circle of Oneness Restored

The Final Vision: The Garden of Oneness

The journey of the Branch finds its perfection here: not in isolation, but in integration. All revelation leads back to the Garden, not of Eden past, but of Zion restored; where God walks once more among living trees, not in the cool of evening only, but in perpetual indwelling light.

> *"I am the true Vine, and My Father is
> the Husbandman." (John 15:1)*

Here, the story completes its circle:

- The Father plants.

- The Son embodies.

- The Spirit flows.

What began as a single seed in Genesis; the Word spoken into dust, has now become a living Vine stretching across eternity.

The Branch has matured into the Vine; the Vine into the Body; the Body into communion. This is the consummation of creation: *God in man, and man in God.*

Theology: The Father as Husbandman — Pruning Not to Wound but to Make Room for Flow

The Father is not a distant overseer but the *intimate Gardener of existence.* His pruning is not punishment but alignment. Every cut He makes is prophetic; it prepares the soul for more light, more fruit, more flow.

In divine horticulture, pruning is an act of mercy. The Gardener removes what drains, not what defines. He touches only the excess that obscures design. Thus, when pain enters a life rooted in God, it is not destruction — it is *divine shaping.*

The Father prunes not to reduce but to *release.* Each branch must make room for new circulation; without the cut, life stagnates. Without surrender, flow ceases.

In this revelation, theology becomes intimacy: the knowledge that every divine touch, even the sharp ones, carries purpose. The Father's hand is both firm and tender, because He sees beyond what we bear now to what we are meant to become.

Spiritology: The Restored Human Spirit Abides by Rhythm, Not Effort — It Breathes with God

The human spirit, once fragmented by rebellion, is now restored to rhythm — *the breath-pattern of divine life.*
To abide is not to labour but to harmonise; not to achieve but to align.

The true vine-life is rhythmic, not mechanical. It flows in seasons of sap; drawing in silence, flowing in word, resting in fruit.

When the Spirit indwells, breathing becomes prayer. Stillness becomes song. The human spirit no longer wrestles with God's will but *resonates* with it. In this rhythm, prayer is not a request but a response; a pulse shared with the Eternal.

Thus, spiritology unveils the law of *spiritual respiration:* to exhale self, to inhale Spirit. To let the breath of the Vine become the breath of the branch.

Here, the Spirit is no longer a visitor; He is the inner current. The soul does not climb to reach God; it abides and lets Him flow through.

Soulogy: The Mind and Heart Learn Surrender as Fruit-Bearing

The mind learns to *trust* the pruning; the heart learns to *rest* in the process. Fruit-bearing is not performance; it is *yielding.* The soul's greatest work is to stop resisting divine rhythm.

In abiding, the will bends without breaking, the emotions flow without flooding, and the intellect perceives without pride.

Soulogy teaches us that surrender is not weakness but wisdom; the art of staying soft in the Gardener's hand.

The soul must learn to love the process more than the product. Every branch that rushes to bear fruit prematurely breaks under its own weight. But the branch that abides, whose root is peace, bears fruit effortlessly, because fruit is not a goal; it is a *consequence of union.*

Thus, the mind becomes Zion, the mountain of divine thought, and the heart becomes Jerusalem; the dwelling of divine feeling. When these unite in surrender, the kingdom within manifests the kingdom without.

Physiology: Divine Life Circulates Through Obedience — Pruning Renews the Nervous and Emotional System Alike

The divine flow is not abstract; it is physiological in manifestation. When the soul aligns with the Spirit, the body aligns with peace. Obedience is the nervous system of the kingdom.

When we resist, our inner currents constrict; when we yield, divine energy circulates freely.

Jesus said, "Every branch that beareth fruit, He purgeth it, that it may bring forth more fruit." (*John 15:2*) This purging renews not only the spiritual state but the *physical vessel.*

Obedience becomes oxygen. The body begins to breathe heaven. The emotional system stabilises, the nervous system calms, the cells remember divine order.

Physiology becomes prophecy; the Vine's sap (Spirit) flowing through every nerve (obedience), healing even the flesh that once resisted.

Typology: The Son as Vine, the Spirit as Sap, the Father as Gardener — The Holy Trinity of Organic Oneness

The mystery of the Vine reveals the hidden triune order:

- **The Father — the Husbandman:** Source and sustainer; the planner of divine ecology.

- **The Son — the Vine:** Structure and substance; the visible embodiment of invisible life.

- **The Spirit — the Sap:** Circulation and communion; the living current that joins all into one body.

This is the *organic Trinity;* not mechanical, not hierarchical, but relational. Each part exists for the other; none can be without the rest.

The Vine is not complete without the Gardener's touch or the Sap's flow. Likewise, creation is not complete until man abides;

the branch restored to its rightful order within this living organism of glory.

In this mystery, redemption reaches its fullness: God is not only worshipped from afar but *experienced from within.* The divine circle closes: Father in Son, Son in Spirit, Spirit in man, man in God.

Application: To Abide Is to Let the Gardener's Hand Define Your Shape; to Resist Is to Dry

Abiding is the art of trust. It is living unguarded under divine care. Every day, the Father walks through His vineyard, pruning, watering, speaking. Those who abide remain tender under His touch.

To abide is to allow God to define your edges; what stays, what goes, what blooms, what waits. To resist is to stiffen, and every stiff branch eventually cracks.

Life in the Vine requires no striving — only *staying.* When the Spirit whispers, respond. When silence comes, rest. When cutting comes, yield. That is how the branch remains green through every season.

Fruitfulness is not achieved; it is received. Those who dwell continually in this circle of oneness discover that every cut is followed by growth, every season of stillness by sap, and every pruning by a fuller glory.

Closing Revelation: The Circle Completed — God All in All

The Vine and the Husbandman is not merely an image of relationship; it is the eternal architecture of divine existence. In it, the story of creation and redemption resolves:

• The Seed of Genesis has grown into the Vine of Revelation.

- The Tree of Life lost in Eden has been replanted in Zion.

- The Branch once bruised is now the Vine that feeds nations.

The circle is complete: **God dwelling in man, and man living in God.** This is the eternal Sabbath; not only a day, but a dimension of being where all labour ceases because all flows.

And in this rest, the voice of the Husbandman echoes through eternity:

"Abide in Me, and I in you… for without Me
ye can do nothing." (John 15:4–5)

The last word of the Vine is not command but communion. The eternal lesson of the Branch is not struggle but surrender. The everlasting fruit is not effort but oneness.

Here, the garden breathes again.
Here the river flows.
Here the Vine and the Husbandman are one, and every branch shines with the same life, the same love, the same light.

Selah — The Circle of Oneness Restored.

PRAYER

for Nationalisation into the
Kingdom of Heaven

Scriptural Foundation:

- *John 3:3 – "Jesus answered and said to him, 'Most assuredly, I say to you, unless one is born again, he cannot see the kingdom of God.'"*

- *Philippians 3:20 – "For our citizenship is in heaven, from which we also eagerly wait for the Savior, the Lord Jesus Christ."*

- *Ephesians 2:19 – "Now therefore you are no longer strangers and foreigners, but fellow citizens with the saints and members of the household of God."*

- *Colossians 1:13 – "He has delivered us from the power of darkness and conveyed us into the kingdom of the Son of His love."*

- *Romans 10:9 – "That if you confess with your mouth the Lord Jesus and believe in your heart that God has raised Him from the dead, you will be saved."*

Righteous Judge of Heaven and Earth,

I come before Your throne, the **throne of Grace** in **the Court of Heaven**, in the name of Jesus Christ, my Lord and Saviour. I stand by the power of His precious blood, which has **redeemed me** and **bought my salvation**. I come humbly and boldly, desiring to be **nationalised into the Kingdom of Heaven**—to become a **true citizen of Your heavenly realm**.

Father, Your Word declares in **John 3:3** that **unless one is born again**, they cannot see the Kingdom of God. Today, **I renounce any citizenship** I once held in this world and any **ties to the powers of darkness**. I acknowledge that I have been **transferred from the kingdom of darkness into the Kingdom of the Son** of Your love (*Colossians 1:13*). I declare that I am no longer a stranger or foreigner, but a **fellow citizen with the saints** and a member of the household of God (*Ephesians 2:19*).

Lord Jesus, I believe with all my heart that You are the **Son of the living God**, that You died for my sins and rose again to grant me eternal life (**Romans 10:9**). I now receive You as my **personal Savior, my Redeemer, the only Way, the Truth**, and **the Life**. You are the **Door to the Father's heart** and the only **path to salvation**. I do not want to **perish** with the world, but to **live eternally with You**.

At this moment, I [Your Full Name] solemnly, sincerely, and truthfully affirm my love, my seriousness, and my desire to follow You and serve You in **holiness and righteousness**. I pledge my full allegiance to You, O King of kings and Lord of lords. I give my loyalty to the third Heaven and honour its **rights and freedoms**. I desire to settle with You, **Lord Jesus**. I repent of the way I have **lived my life and of all my sins**. Take over **my heart and my destiny**. Save me, cleanse me, and change me.

I beseech that You **seal my heavenly citizenship today**. Let the record of **my new identity** be **registered in the Court of Heaven**. Write my name in the **Lamb's Book of Life**, and erase it from the **book of death and judgment**. Let every **legal claim the enemy** has over my past be **cancelled** and **rendered powerless by the blood of Jesus**.

Lord, I am ready to walk the path of **righteousness and holiness**. I cast all **my cares and all of myself upon You**, for You care for me and loved me and laid Your life as the Lamb slain from **the foundation of the world**. Let Your **will be done** in my life as it is in Heaven.

By Your blood, I now receive eternal life. I proclaim that I am a **new creature**. By the word of Your testimony, I am made free indeed. **Fill me and baptize me** with the **Holy Ghost and fire**. Thank You, Lord Jesus, for giving me the right and the power to become a child of God, born **not of flesh but of the Spirit**, according to **the new covenant sealed in Your blood**.

I believe **You died** for me, and on the **third day**, You rose again. You are now seated at the right hand of the **Father in glory**, and I receive You as the Lord of my life. Through You, I have **received grace, peace, forgiveness, and eternal inheritance**. I stand holy, blameless, and without fault before the **Court of Heaven** because of the **righteousness imputed to me through Your sacrifice**.

Now, I **declare that the power of sin, death, and Satan— including the grave**—has been **broken over my life**. I walk in the eternal victory of the Cross. From this day forward, I will never look back. Backward—never. Forward—forever.

Degree and Declare: I am a citizen of Heaven. I live for Your Kingdom. **I walk in Your authority and power**. I receive the **full inheritance of health, peace, righteousness, Wealth, and provision, even eternal life**.

In Jesus' mighty name, I pray.

Amen.

EPILOGUE

The Return of the Fruitful Ones

There comes a moment in every generation when God calls His sons out of obscurity.
Not with noise, but with knowing.
Not with spectacle, but with sight.

This is that moment.

All throughout history, the Father has guarded a remnant branches hidden beneath the noise of nations, preserved in silence, strengthened in secret. Their roots wrapped around the eternal Vine while the world rushed past them unaware.

But the seasons have shifted.
The hour has changed.
The vineyard of the earth is entering its final audit.

The last pruning has begun.

And in this sacred transition, the fruitful ones emerge.

They do not rise with arrogance.
They rise with accuracy.
They move with clarity.
They build with understanding.

Because they know the source.
They know the flow.

They know the blueprint.

They know the Vine.

Everything this book has unveiled
the architecture of identity,
the intelligence of the Vein,
the majesty of the Root,
the dignity of the Branch has been preparation for this single
mandate:

Bear fruit that remains.

Not fruit of effort, but fruit of alignment.
Not fruit of ambition, but fruit of abiding.
Not fruit for applause, but fruit for dominion.

The world is shifting toward turbulence.
Systems will shake.
Institutions will fracture.
False vines will collapse under their own weight.

But those connected to the living Root will stand.
And not merely stand; they will overflow.

This is the legacy of the Vine.
This is the brilliance of the Vein.
This is the inheritance of the Branch.

Let this epilogue be your quiet commissioning:
carry the life of God with integrity, govern your sphere with
wisdom, saturate your environment with the fragrance of the
Root, and let your fruit speak where words fail.

The Father is walking through His garden again.
He is searching for branches that reflect His design.
He is calling for sons whose lives echo eternity.

May you be counted among them.
May you be found fruitful.

May you abide until the end.

For the Vine endures.
The Vein flows.
And the Branch lives.

Forever.

AFTERWORD

*When the Branch Stands,
the World Turns*

Every journey that begins in revelation must end in responsibility.
Every unveiling demands a response.
Every awakening carries an assignment.

You have walked through the Vine, followed the pulse of the Vein, and recognised the dignity of the Branch.
Now the question rises like morning light:

What will you do with what you have become?

Identity is not a concept.
Identity is capacity.
It is the vessel through which heaven delivers its intentions into the earth.

The Branch is not ornamental.
The Branch is operational.

It bears fruit.
It stabilises atmospheres.
It becomes a living extension of the Root's intelligence, executing the counsel of God in real time.

This book was never written to be an end.
It was written to be a gate.

A gate into alignment.
A gate into inheritance.
A gate into sonship expressed with clarity, stability, and authority.

Now the architecture belongs to you.

You carry a Vine that cannot die,
a Vein that cannot corrupt,
a Root that cannot fail, and a destiny that cannot be delayed by human systems or spiritual resistance.

Your assignment is not to strive; but to flow.
Not to force; but to abide.
Not to impress; but to embody.

The world is entering a season where borrowed identities will collapse, where artificial vines will wither, and where fruitless systems will expose themselves under the pressure of time.
But the sons of Zion; those who stand as true branches—
will remain.

And more than remain: they will govern.

This is your moment to root deeply, to grow steadily, to lift your crown quietly, and to let the world taste the life of God through the fruit you bear.

The Root has spoken.
The Vein has flowed.
The Vine has stretched its arms across time.

Now the Branch rises.

If this book has done anything,
let it be this:
that when the wind blows,
you will not bend in confusion
you will stand in identity.

Because when the Branch stands, the world turns.

ACKNOWLEDGEMENT

To the God who is both Architect and Atmosphere, thank You for the revelation that breathes through every page.
Your wisdom is the root system beneath every insight here.

To Jesus Christ, the Vine eternal, thank You for the life that flows unbroken, for the covenant blood that became our Vein of truth, and for the invitation to abide in a glory older than creation.

To the Holy Spirit, the Sabbath within us, the Rest that governs us, the Breath that trains sons into kings.
Your whisper opened the chambers.

To the sons and daughters awakening across nations, those who hear the faint hum of destiny in their bones: your hunger shaped the urgency of this work.
May the revelation in these pages strengthen your posture in Zion.

And to every teacher, seeker, intercessor, and builder, who carries the burden of restoring God's ancient pathways, this book honours your labour.
Your devotion is a seed in God's garden.

ABOUT THE AUTHOR

Anthony Mwangi — The Branch Seated In Zion

Anthony Mwangi is a prophetic architect of revelation, a teacher of spiritual identity, and a steward of mysteries rooted in the ancient counsel of God. His work carries a distinct assignment: to restore original design, rebuild the inner structures of sonship, and awaken the royal lineage hidden within the sons of Zion.

He writes with the precision of a strategist and the fire of a seer; drawing from the Vine, flowing through the Vein, and manifesting the inheritance of the Branch. His teachings merge prophetic insight, scriptural depth, and spiritual intelligence, forming a blueprint that reorients believers toward their eternal identity.

Anthony's writings have become a body of work marked by purity, clarity, and undiluted truth. His books—recorded in the spirit as writings of fire, are engineered to shift atmospheres, recalibrate foundations, and activate the divine architecture within all who read them.

Functioning under a mantle of revelation and rest, he draws from the ancient patterns of Zion to build frameworks that restore order in an age of confusion. His voice is a trumpet for alignment, a call to return to the Root, and a witness to the unfolding of God's design in the last days.

Through every book, teaching, and prophetic commission, Anthony Mwangi stands as a Branch in full expression—rooted in Christ, governed by the Spirit, and committed to raising sons who bear fruit that remains.

BOOKS BY THIS AUTHOR

The Marriage Supper Of The Lamb: The Final War Of Love

Heaven has an order. Love has a government. The Lamb has a strategy.

In this groundbreaking prophetic work, The Marriage Supper of the Lamb: The Final War of Love, Anthony Mwangi unveils the hidden architecture of the end-time covenant between Christ and His Bride. More than a celebration, the Marriage Supper is revealed as Heaven's ultimate act of war — where intimacy becomes victory and union becomes dominion.

Drawing from the 7-Dimensional Word of God, the 3 Modes of Revelation, and a detailed study of 18 biblical marriages + 7 prophetic weddings, this book exposes God's protocol for the last days: how the Lamb wins by sacrifice, how the Lion reigns by fire, and how the Bride rises to rule with Him in eternal covenant.

Readers will discover:

The divine protocol behind all revelation — precept upon precept, line upon line

Why the Marriage Supper is an ordered decree of judgment, glory, and love

The supernatural patterns behind biblical unions and how they reveal Christ's final victory

The role of the Bride in the end-time war of worship, fire, purity, and rest

How Heaven structures intimacy, government, and dominion

The mystery of the Lamb and the Lion in the same Christ

The prophetic meaning of garments, oil, trumpets, tables, crowns, and sceptres

What it truly means to sit at the King's table at the end of the age

With poetic revelation and airtight prophetic logic, Mwangi guides the reader step-by-step — from Genesis unions to Revelation's wedding — unveiling how every covenant, sacrifice, feast, and throne room moment points toward one climactic event: the eternal joining of the Lamb and His Bride in the Final War of Love.

Whether you are a pastor, intercessor, theologian, prophetic teacher, or hungry believer, this book will transform your understanding of the end times, awaken your identity as the Bride, and align you with Heaven's strategy for the last battle.

The table is set.
The sceptre is extended.
The crown is prepared.
The Bride is rising.

Step into the revelation. Step into the war. Step into the Supper.

The Armour Of Light: Unlocking The Mystery Of

Divine Warfare

In the last days, the battlefield is no longer fought with swords and spears, but with light, truth, and the Spirit. The Armour of Light: Unlocking the Mystery of Divine Warfare is a prophetic unveiling of God's end-time strategy for His chosen remnant.

This masterpiece reveals the hidden dimensions of the Word of God and the power of the Holy Spirit as the true armour that clothes, protects, and empowers the believer. Through spiritology, soulogy, physiology, and theology, the mystery of warfare is unfolded—showing how the Sabbath is God's dwelling place, the Courtroom of Heaven is His battlefield, and the Bride is His warrior.

Drawing from ancient truths and prophetic revelations, Anthony Mwangi — the BRANCH seated in Zion — uncovers the role of man in God's eternal judgment, the secret of Christ's blood as the light of warfare, and the revelation of the 7-dimensional Word as the weapon that disarms the dragon, the beast, and the false prophet.

This book is not just a teaching, but a weapon in itself. It equips the end-time believer to stand clothed in fire, sealed by the Spirit, and ready to triumph in the last battle.

If you are called to be part of the remnant, this is your manual of divine warfare.

The True Church (Ekklesia): The Undisputed Government Of Heaven On Earth

The Church was never designed to be a passive audience. It was crafted to be a governing body; Heaven's operational command centre on the earth.

This prophetic masterpiece unveils the Church in her original mandate: a ruling, legislative, fire-crowned government seated in Christ, built to administer righteousness, execute divine justice, and steward the expansion of the Kingdom with unshakeable authority.

Moving beyond institutional religion, this book repositions the reader inside the architectural blueprint of God's eternal design, where the Ekklesia stands as Heaven's governing senate, the Lamb's undefeated Heavyweight Government operating in light, truth, and dominion.

Each chapter pulls you deeper into the designer realm of the Word, where identity becomes structure and revelation becomes strategy. You will discover:

The true governmental nature of the Church
How sons legislate from Zion through rest, not striving
Why hell cannot contend with a people aligned to the Throne
How the 7-Dimensional Word of God equips believers for rule
The rise of Kingdom coalitions, watchtowers, and councils
The architecture of divine order that establishes peace without end
This is not just a teaching; it is a governmental activation. A call to rise, build, legislate, and stand in your ordained post within Heaven's expanding Kingdom.

For reformers, intercessors, apostolic builders, prophetic architects, and every believer hungry to move beyond survival into governance, this book is your blueprint.

Step into the council.
Stand in the light.
Take your seat in the Undisputed Government of the Lamb.

Who Is Jesus? (The Whirring Children: A 12-Book Series 1)

WHO IS JESUS? — Meeting Jesus for the First Time

Introduce your child to the love of Jesus in a gentle, tender way with Who Is Jesus? This beautifully illustrated story helps children meet Jesus for the very first time and understand that He is always with them.

Through this book, your child will:

✓ Discover a Simple Gospel Story — A story of love, kindness, courage, and hope, brought to life with vivid imagery for young imaginations.

✓ Learn Their First Memory Verse — A small seed of Scripture planted in the heart, laying the foundation for a lifelong relationship with God.

✓ Say Their First Prayer of Belonging — A pure, simple prayer that teaches children to give their hearts to Jesus.

✓ Enjoy Daily "Talk With Jesus" Activities — Tiny, meaningful moments each day that help children speak with Jesus as naturally as they breathe.

Perfect for parents, grandparents, and caregivers who want to nurture faith, wonder, and a personal connection with God in young hearts. Start your child's journey with Jesus today!

The Message From Jesus Christ Return: Return, O Israel

A Prophetic Warning. A Heavenly Invitation. A Call to the Remnant.

The Message from Jesus Christ: RETURN, O ISRAEL is not merely a book; it is a divine summons. Delivered through The Lord Jesus Christ Himself, given scripture, revelation, and the voice of the Spirit, this work carries a message the Lord Jesus Christ is giving to this generation: Return. Awaken. Prepare.

Across powerful precepts drawn directly from the Word of God, this book unveils the urgency of Christ's soon coming, the restoration of Israel's true spiritual identity, and the gathering of God's scattered sons from every nation. From Isaiah to Zephaniah, Ezekiel to Matthew, each passage is opened through a prophetic lens using the 3M (spoken, written, vision) + 7D model — a unique Spirit-breathed method for interpreting scripture in these last days.

The message is clear:
The King is at the door. The nations tremble. The churches must awaken. And Israel must return to her God.

You will discover:

The true meaning of the Great Day of the LORD

Why God is calling His remnant out of the nations

The spiritual identity and awakening of Israel in our time

How Christ Himself is summoning His people through scripture

The prophetic significance of the present generation

How to stand ready for the Second Coming with purity and understanding

More than a warning, this is an invitation — from Jesus Christ Himself — to come out of confusion, return to covenant identity, and align with heaven's final movement.

Whether you are a believer seeking clarity, a watchman longing to understand the times, or a seeker drawn by the Spirit, this book will stir your soul, awaken your spirit, and ignite a deeper devotion to the King of Kings.

The Spirit and the Bride say, Come.
Even so, Lord Jesus, come quickly.

The Issue Of The Horse: The Courtroom Indictment Against Easter, Christmas, And Modern Pagan Feasts

In a generation reshaped by convenience, tradition, and cultural drift, what if the greatest spiritual compromise is hiding in plain sight?

This book issues a bold, courtroom-level challenge to the most celebrated religious holidays: Easter, Christmas, and the modern feasts that carry the fingerprints of Babylon more than the signature of God.

Drawing from prophetic insight, forensic Scripture analysis, and the ancient protocols of the Holy Spirit, The Issue of the Horse unmasks the systems that led believers away from covenant identity and into ritual mixtures dressed as worship. It reveals how syncretism infiltrated the church, how altars were exchanged, and why heaven's court is calling for a return to purity.

This is not a rant. It's a verdict.

A clear, uncompromising case built line upon line—rooted in the King James Bible, reinforced by historical evidence, and charged with a future-focused mandate: to realign the body of Christ with the original statutes of the Spirit.

Readers will discover:

The prophetic meaning of "the horse" and how it exposes counterfeit worship

Why certain feasts carry a spiritual indictment

How the courtroom of heaven evaluates worship, sacrifice, and alignment

The clash between the Holy Spirit's Sabbath identity and modern religious tradition

The call of Zion for believers to return to covenant rest and Spirit-governed truth

This book is a wake-up call for believers, leaders, intercessors, and truth-seekers who know something is off but have lacked the language, evidence, and prophetic clarity to name it.

If you're ready to confront the mixture, reclaim ancient order, and stand in the firelight of truth,step into the courtroom.
The Spirit has issued a summons.
The verdict is unfolding.
And the remnant is rising.

Sabbath: The Name Of The Holy Spirit — God's Covenant Protocol For The Last Days

This book unveils a groundbreaking revelation: the Sabbath is the Name, Seal, and Rest of the Holy Spirit, and the end-time Church cannot walk in covenant power without understanding this identity. Drawing from the 7-Dimensional Word of God, this work decodes the Sabbath as God's ancient–future protocol — the original sign of His presence, the governing code of His kingdom, and the prophetic mark that distinguishes His remnant in the last days.

You will discover how the Sabbath reveals God's hidden Name, aligns the mind with divine order, and positions the body as the dwelling place where the Spirit rests. From Eden's first seventh-day revelation to the sealed remnant of Revelation, this book demonstrates that to hallow the Sabbath is to hallow His Name, and that the restoration of Sabbath order is the restoration of God's government on earth.

Packed with visionary insights, prophetic typology, and a full blueprint for spiritual formation, this book equips believers to:

Understand the Sabbath as the signature identity of the Holy Spirit

Discern the covenant seal that separates truth from deception in the last days

Rebuild the altar of rest in the mind, heart, and body

Walk in the rhythm, protection, and judgment of God's kingdom order

Stand in Zion as those who have entered His Rest

This is not merely theology — it is kingdom strategy.
A call to return.
A summons to alignment.
A preparation for the remnant.

SABBATH: The Name of the Holy Spirit is your guide to reclaiming God's original covenant protocol, and stepping into the Rest that marks His people for the final generation.

Stars From The East (Irathiro)

The Scroll of Irathiro: The Rising Light from the East
By Anthony Mwangi — The BRANCH Seated in Zion

From the snows of Mount Kenya to the throne of eternal fire, The Scroll of Irathiro unveils a prophetic revelation hidden for generations. This masterpiece carries the light of divine remembrance — a message to restore identity, awaken the remnant, and call nations back to covenant truth.

Through the 7-Dimensional Word of God and the Spirit's rhythm of revelation, the author unfolds mysteries connecting ancient prophecy, African identity, and the returning glory of Christ — the King whose hair is white as wool and whose eyes burn with eternal purpose.

Each chapter breathes with vision and fire: from the golden offerings of the Magi to the judgment of nations, from the altar of Zion to the rivers of counsel flowing from the throne. It is not merely a book — it is a scroll of destiny, written in light and sealed in blood.

Those who read will find themselves within the story of restoration — called to stand as witnesses in the Court of Heaven, bearing the sign of the covenant and the song of the East.

Prophetic. Powerful. Undiluted truth.
This is not history retold — it is prophecy fulfilled.

Deliverance By Fire: Unlocking The Courts, Thrones, And Altars Of True Freedom

A 7-Dimensional Manual for Self-Deliverance and Exorcism Ministry
By Anthony Mwangi — The BRANCH Seated in Zion

This prophetic manual is not just a teaching — it is a spiritual courtroom, an altar of judgment, and a throne of fire. Deliverance by Fire unveils the divine order of freedom as legislated in heaven's courts and manifested through the Spirit of Truth on earth.

Within these pages, you will encounter the architecture of true deliverance:
the Courts of Heaven, where accusations are silenced;
the Thrones of Dominion, where believers reign in Christ;
and the Altars of Fire, where covenants are purified and destinies reborn.

Built upon the revelation of the Seven Spirits of God, this book exposes the counterfeit thrones of darkness — and trains the sons and daughters of Zion to war by decree, not emotion; by the Word, not the flesh. Each chapter blends courtroom insight, prophetic instruction, and altar-based declarations to forge warriors of holiness and rest.

Through this 7-dimensional model — Spiritology, Soulogy, Physiology, Theology, Chronology, Typology, and Technology — Anthony Mwangi reveals how the Spirit of Judgment and Burning restores divine order, purges bloodlines, and reclaims the altars of families, cities, and nations.

This book will teach you to:

Minister deliverance through heavenly legal protocol.

Break bloodline covenants and generational curses with the fire of truth.

Build Sabbath altars that sustain freedom and spiritual authority.

Operate in the courts of Zion, where Christ is both Judge and Advocate.

Move from manifestation to dominion — from reaction to legislation.

Deliverance by Fire is more than deliverance — it is reformation. It is the blueprint of how heaven reclaims the earth through purified vessels who have become living stones and burning altars of the Spirit.

When you finish reading, you will not just understand deliverance — you will embody it.

Authority Over The Seven Demonic Nations

A Spiritual Eviction Manual for Gatekeepers is a prophetic warfare guide designed to expose and overthrow the ancient strongholds that still occupy the gates of your life, family, and inheritance.

Based on Joshua 3:10, this book reveals the spiritual identities behind the seven Canaanite nations—territorial powers that God commanded to be driven out. These are not just historical enemies; they are legal systems of defilement, fear, deception, generational bondage, pride, rejection, and dream manipulation.

Each nation is prophetically aligned with a ruling throne from the kingdom of darkness:

Canaanites – Lust / Defilement (Asmodeus)

Hittites – Wrath / Fear (Satan)

Hivites – Envy / Deception (Leviathan)

Perizzites – Sloth / Instability (Belphegor)

Girgashites – Greed / Ancestral Curses (Mammon)

Amorites – Pride / Domination (Lucifer)

Jebusites – Shame / Mockery (Beelzebub)

Through deep biblical revelation, courtroom language, and prophetic teaching, this manual will help you:

Identify the strongmen ruling over key gates in your life

Break legal rights and generational covenants that empower them

Rebuild spiritual altars and secure your inheritance

Activate your calling as a Gatekeeper in these last days

Pray elite-level courtroom decrees to dismantle demonic thrones

Whether you're a deliverance minister, prophetic intercessor, or believer hungry for spiritual authority, this book equips you to evict the enemy legally, spiritually, and permanently.

The thrones must fall. Your gates must be restored. Your territory must be cleansed.

www.ingramcontent.com/pod-product-compliance
Lightning Source LLC
LaVergne TN
LVHW051235080426
835513LV00016B/1597